Soho

Soho

The Heart of Bohemian London

Peter Speiser

BRITISH LIBRARY

First published in 2017 by
The British Library
96 Euston Road
London NW1 2DB

British Library Cataloguing in Publication Data A catalogue record for this book is available from the British Library

ISBN: 978 0 7123 5657 2

Frontispiece: 'The Café Royalists: The "Mixture as Before"'. Illustration by Dorothea St George, in Horace Wyndham, *Nights in London: Where Mayfair Makes Merry*, 1926.

Typeset by IDSUK (DataConnection) Ltd
Cover by Sandra Friesen Design
Picture research by Sally Nicholls
Printed in Italy by Lego S.p.A.

Contents

'I. Street Scene. II. In Little Crown Court. III. An 8d Table d'Hote (with Facsimile of Menu). IV. Sunday Morning Shopping.' Plate depicting Soho scenes, in G. R. Sims (ed.), *Living London, Its Work and its Play. Its Humour and its Pathos. Its Sights and its Scenes,* Cassell 1901.

Chapter 1   Introducing Soho

At the end of the nineteenth century, the novelist and playwright John Galsworthy described Soho as 'untidy, full of Greeks, Ishmaelites, cats, Italians, tomatoes, restaurants, organs, coloured stuffs, queer names, people looking out of upper windows, it dwells remote from the British Body Politic'.[1] This impression was echoed by Thomas Burke's 1915 work *Nights in London Town*: 'Soho – magic syllables! For when the respectable Londoner wants to feel devilish he goes to Soho, where every street is a song. He walks through Old Compton Street and instinctively he swaggers; he is abroad; he is a dog.'[2] This book tells the story of one of London's most famous, cosmopolitan, colourful and notorious neighbourhoods.

Burke's portrayal of Soho at the beginning of the First World War neatly sums up some of the main facets of Soho's character, with its reference to the cosmopolitan nature of the district where traditionally the French but increasingly also Jewish, Italian, German, Swiss and other communities dominated. By providing a view of Soho as a place to 'feel devilish', Burke is also making reference to the growing social and cultural importance of the area.

It may well be that part of Soho's allure has been the mystery surrounding the district. Even its exact boundaries have been disputed throughout its history. Often, but not always, they include the eastern parts of St James's and thereby push westwards to Regent Street; sometimes they even incorporate streets just to the north of Oxford Street. In the late 1950s Colin MacInnes, in anticipation of the social changes of Swinging London, saw Soho as a place where 'all the things they say happen, do'.[3] By the 1960s Soho, despite its transformation to a place of business, still had 'an atmosphere not to be found anywhere else in London ... There are so many sides to Soho and so many things going on that it is difficult to know where to begin'.[4] This book aims to discover the many layers of the history of one of London's most remarkable areas by looking at its streets, its businesses, Soho's world of entertainment and, last but not least, the people who brought the area to worldwide fame.

Fashionable Origins

Throughout its history Soho has attracted many of London's most remarkable inhabitants and visitors, including royalty, artists and artisans. The story begins in the seventeenth century with the ill-fated James Scott, Duke of Monmouth, the favourite illegitimate son of Charles II (after the failure of his attempt to depose his uncle, King James II, he was beheaded for treason in 1685). Briefly residing in Monmouth House, the Duke was responsible for Soho Square becoming one of the most fashionable addresses in town as early as the 1680s.

Over the years the square continued to attract colourful residents – such as Theresa Cornelys. Also known as Madame de Trenti and La Pompeati, the former singer and one-time lover of Casanova completely transformed the nature of London's evening entertainment. Her 'Society of Soho Square' attracted the wealthiest of London's nobility and gentry with its wild masquerades and balls. Fanny Burney, another of Soho's famous residents, wrote in 1770 that 'the magnificence of the rooms, splendour of the illuminations and embellishments, and the brilliant appearance of the company exceeded anything I ever saw before'. Casanova himself recalled after a visit that 'the ball

'Soho Square 1700'. Engraving in W. Thornbury, *Old & New London*, Cassell 1898.

'Remarkable Characters at Mrs Cornely's Masquerade'. Plate from *The Oxford Magazine, or Universal Museum. ...*, 1711.

'Mademoiselle de Beaumont, or the Chevalier d'Éon, Female Minister Plenipo. Capt. of Dragoons &c, &c.' Plate from *The London Magazine*, September 1777.

lasted all night without ceasing, as the company ate by relays, and at all times and hours; the waste and prodigality were worthy of a prince's palace. I made the acquaintance of all the nobility, and the Royal Family, for they were all there, with the exception of the king and queen, and the Prince of Wales'.[5]

Soho's close connection with the royal family had been cemented when Leicester House began to serve as refuge to the sons of both George I and George II in the first half of the eighteenth century. Leicester Fields (now Leicester Square) was thereby transformed into the centre of London's social scene. Prime Minister Robert Walpole commented that 'the most promising of the young lords and gentlemen . . . and the prettiest and liveliest of the young ladies, formed a new Court of the Prince and Princess of Wales. The apartment of the bed-chamber-woman in waiting became the fashionable evening rendezvous of the most distinguished wits and beauties'. Prominent neighbours included Sir Isaac Newton, who moved to Soho in 1711.

Other notorious eighteenth-century residents of Soho included the Chevalier d'Éon, French Minister Plenipotentiary. A man who liked to dress as a woman, he coined the term 'eonism', meaning transvestism. He resided in Soho in the 1760s before returning to France – as a woman – only to return to Soho and to spend the rest of her life there as the Chevalière d'Éon.

Changing Fortunes

Soho's status as the most fashionable area of London began to wane in the mid-eighteenth century with the departure of many aristocrats to the even larger mansions of Mayfair. The decline of the area was, however, a slow one, and it did not make Soho less attractive to its notable inhabitants. Even as poverty increased, the attraction of the area remained.

Best-remembered for the *Swallows and Amazons* series of children's books, Arthur Ransome's first publishing success,

'A Court for King Cholera'. Cartoon by John Leech from *Punch*, 25 September 1852..

in 1907, was the evocatively titled *Bohemia in London*. In it, he wrote:

> And all over Soho are . . . small meeting places, where irregulars of all sorts flock to lunch and dine . . . Still, in some of the upper windows may be seen the glitter of a candle-light where a scholar, probably foreign, pores over a book in the hours when the British Museum is closed to him. And in a hundred of the small rooms in the piles of Soho flats, small rooms furnished with a bed, a chair, and a table that also serves for a washing-stand, are there young actors and actresses, studying great parts and playing small ones. . .[6]

Soho's decline into a poverty-stricken and decaying Victorian hub of cheap lodging houses had attracted ever new groups of penniless residents from London and the wider world. This was the Soho of the devastating cholera outbreak of 1854, witnessed by the anaesthetist and epidemiologist Dr John Snow. His observations in the area eventually enabled him to establish the real cause of the disease (discussed in more detail in chapter 5). This was also the Soho where the exiled revolutionary Karl Marx, according to a Prussian agent who visited him, lived in 'one of the worst, and hence the cheapest quarters of London'. In the nineteenth century the population of the area increased rapidly, and by 1851 there were 327 inhabitants per acre, a figure higher than in almost any other area of London. Houses were divided into tenements, and overcrowding was common. Long after he had exchanged his Soho flat for a home in the leafy suburb of Primrose Hill, Karl Marx recalled that 'the region round Soho Square still sends a shiver down my spine if I happen to be anywhere near there'.[7]

However, the departure of the wealthiest inhabitants and the increase of immigration led to a new focus on business and manufacturing – which was to transform Soho in the late nineteenth and twentieth centuries. Alongside this, bars and restaurants flourished, encouraging artists and artisans to the area. One resident of Fitzrovia remembered n the 1930s that:

> the people who came from Soho seemed racier . . . more street wise than we were. I could tell the difference between the Soho people and us. I can't put my finger exactly on the difference, but it revealed itself in their demeanour, their street language, that sort of thing. Because they lived in Soho, prostitution was on every street corner and the snooker halls were on their doorstep, not ours. And they were bunking into the cinemas through the back door every day of the week.[8]

Three decades later, for a brief moment in the 1960s, Carnaby Street – one of the most run-down streets of inter-war Soho – became the fashion and retail centre of the world. Post-war British youth culture became an integral part of Soho, with coffee bars and nightclubs playing host to the Teds, Mods, Rockers, Punks and New Romantics.

*　*　*

This book aims to shed new light on aspects of Soho's diverse history by focusing on the urban fabric, as well as some of the people and communities who shaped the area, from the Victorian era to the 1950s. The next chapter, exploring some of Soho's streets and squares in detail, recalls the lives of the numerous communities of Soho – many with French, Italian and Jewish backgrounds, but also those from Switzerland, Sweden, Greece, Germany, China and of course Britain. A focus on its buildings evokes the exciting nightlife and entertainment of the area. The incredible diversity of Soho's people and history becomes apparent when delving into the histories of individual streets, squares and even individual houses.

Much of Soho's eighteenth- and nineteenth-century housing stock was well past its prime by the early twentieth century. One resident recalled that:

> they weren't so much cold as draughty. They had high ceilings, and the windows and doors didn't fit properly. If you sat in front of the fire your front was scorched and your back was freezing, and you had chilblains when you went to bed . . . When the house was demolished they found the most beautiful panelling underneath, which was sold for a fortune to America. So it had been a good house once – which is why it had an indoor loo.[9]

The ups and downs in Soho's fortunes are often reflected by who is inhabiting the buildings at a given time. One Sohoite was born in the house that had been occupied by poet, painter and visionary, William Blake, in the nineteenth century. By 1919 it had become a tenement that was occupied by two families, with the top floor let out as tailoring workshops: 'My family lived on the first floor – seven people in three small rooms – one room acting as living room and workroom combined, containing the last vestiges of grandeur of the prestigious former occupants, in the shape of two built-in glass fronted cupboards one either side of the fireplace – our library.'[10] Overcrowding was so much a part of Soho life that it was common to see signs in the windows of the old houses advertising 'part of a room to let'.[11]

The third chapter shows how ordinary Sohoites who lived in these houses and streets went about earning a living throughout the nineteenth and twentieth centuries. One of the trades most often associated with the area is prostitution, and this was indeed one of the most visible features of Soho until the mid-twentieth century. The artist Francis Bacon, describing Soho in the 1950s, recalled that 'the prostitutes were all over the streets. The streets were more fun, more amusing. The prostitutes gave a living sense to the streets'.[12] This chapter highlights how Soho was shaped by the world's oldest trade. One of Soho's earliest residents, a 'lewd

Two prostitutes lean out of the windows of a brothel in Soho. Photograph by Thurston Hopkins, published in 'I am the Queen of Soho', *Picture Post*, 1956.

woman' named Anna Clerke, was recorded as 'threateninge to burne the houses at So:ho' in 1641. Her presence was followed by high-class courtesans such as Elizabeth Price of Frith Street, 'a Player and mistress to several persons', and Elizabeth Flint, 'generally slut and drunkard; occasionally whore and thief', who resided in Meard Street in the 1750s.[13] Attitudes towards prostitution in the seventeenth and eighteenth centuries were in stark contrast to those of the Victorian era. Prostitutes operated freely, and mistresses were openly acknowledged. A number of high-class brothels existed in Soho such as the notorious 'White House', which in the late 1770s was frequented by George, Prince of Wales.

The nature of prostitution changed drastically in the nineteenth century, when it became either a dire necessity for thousands of destitute women with no other means of support, or the only alternative to the irregular, monotonous, low-paid and often dangerous work available to working-class women in London's East End. Despite all philanthropic attempts to eradicate prostitution, including those of Prime Minister Gladstone who had invited prostitutes into his house to convince them of their erring ways, Edwardian Soho has been described as the 'world's largest flesh market, its streets after dark almost entirely given over to sexual commerce'.[14]

One of Soho's most infamous gangs, the five Messina brothers, originally from Malta, established a network of brothels in Soho and Mayfair in the 1930s. Bernie Silver, one of their henchmen, quickly earned himself the nickname 'The Godfather of Soho'. By the late 1950s Silver and his fellow gangster 'Big Frank' Mifsud had established a sophisticated network of prostitutes, gambling dens and striptease clubs throughout the West End, which was run from an office in Romilly Street. They had the Soho underworld well and truly under their control, with the help of police officers and Scotland Yard detectives whom they bribed on a massive scale. But they were only some of the most prominent of Soho's gangsters, and this chapter shows just how closely connected Soho's underworld was to London's rich and famous.

Despite the prominence of the sex industry, thousands of ordinary people in the area pursued many other trades and businesses which gave Soho its unique atmosphere. Its position just off Oxford Street attracted businesses such as local food manufacturers Crosse & Blackwell, whose large factory operated in Soho Square until the 1920s. Soho Square also witnessed the opening of London's first department store in 1816, the Soho Bazaar. Opened by businessman John Trotter, the bazaar's philanthropic aim was to allow 'the industrious . . . to thrive; reduced tradesmen may recover and retain their connexions; beginners may form connexions and habits, before they encounter more expensive speculations'. The bazaar was still in operation some eighty years later. By 1900 practically every industry and retail business had a foothold in Soho, including food producers, billiard-table makers, silversmiths, clock makers, carpenters and furniture makers, musical instrument makers and music printers, book publishers and book dealers.

Chapter 4 explores the colourful history of entertainment by exploring Soho's theatres and music halls, including the famous Alhambra in Leicester Square which was replaced in 1936 with the iconic art deco Odeon cinema. Soho's history of entertainment also entails some of the more unusual establishments in the area, such as Wyld's Monster Globe. Erected in the then overgrown and dilapidated centre of Leicester Square in 1851, the year of the Great Exhibition, it was inspired by the Liberal MP and geographer James Wyld. The large rotunda housed a huge circular globe, 'a great model of the earth's surface', 60 feet in diameter, which allowed sightseers to gaze at the 'physical features of the earth'.[15]

Towards the end of the nineteenth century there was a remarkable change in the habits of London society, with

'The Building in Leicester-Square, for Mr. Wyld's Model of the Earth.' Plate in the *Illustrated London News*, 29 March 1851.

public restaurants being used for the first time for luncheon and supper occasions that would have previously taken place in the home. This change in social habits, combined with the building of new theatres in Shaftesbury Avenue and Charing Cross Road, transformed the hitherto dingy and often second-rate eating-houses of Soho. In the period after the First World War, when the decline in the number of domestic servants led to an increase in eating out, Soho's gastronomic reputation was finally established. During the 1920s and 1930s restaurants such as Berlemont's, above the bar of the York Minster pub, were frequented by the Prince of Wales, 'usually with 'a beautiful wench on either arm' and Lord Beaverbrook, who had 'more nieces than any man'. At the Gargoyle Club in Meard Street, or the Café de Paris in Coventry Street, the party at the next table regularly included film stars, actresses, band-leaders, sports people or royalty.

Soho's Windmill Theatre caused a storm with its displays of nudity, thereby contributing to the popularity and notoriety of the area. From around the turn of the twentieth century, Soho was also frequently associated with London's so-called Bohemians, with favourite haunts frequented by the likes of Oscar Wilde, George Bernard Shaw, H. G. Wells, Max Beerbohm and Walter Sickert. Drawn together by a shared love of good talk, good champagne, outlandish behaviour, artistic interests and, in some cases, homosexuality, not surprisingly their favourite place in Soho was the Café Royal. This infamous venue was later frequented by artists such as Lucian Freud and John Minton. But Soho's pubs were equally important. The Coach and Horses and the York Minster were only two of the many centres of the Soho drinking set.

The pursuit of pleasure, the arts and music during years of war and peace is highlighted in Chapter 5, through the perspectives and stories of Soho's more famous residents. Comedians from Peter Sellers to Morecambe and Wise, painters such as Freud, Minton and Francis Bacon, writers such as Colin MacInnes

'Leicester Square About 1750.' Engraving from W. Thornbury, Old & London, Cassell 1898.

and George Melly, musicians such as Tommy Steele and Cliff Richard, are just some examples from a long list of famous artists who shaped the history of Soho. This list also of course includes many royals, diplomats and politicians who spent some of their time in Soho.

In addition, Soho's history is inextricably linked with that of London's immigration. The cosmopolitan character of the area goes back to the humble beginnings of Soho, when French Huguenots left their mark. They were joined by Italians after the tumultuous *Risorgimento* of the 1860s, and then soon afterwards by Jews escaping pogroms in Russia and Eastern Europe. By the early twentieth century Germans had also arrived, many of them cooks and waiters, together with considerable numbers of Greeks and Swiss. This chapter therefore looks at the impact of the immigrant communities on the area, including the plight of the Italian and German communities during the two world wars and also the development of Chinatown.

To conclude this journey through Soho's history, the final chapter looks at the impact of 200 years on the present and the future, celebrating the enduring qualities of this extraordinary area of London.

But now it is time to take a tour through some of the streets and squares of Soho, and to pay a brief visit to some of its residences.

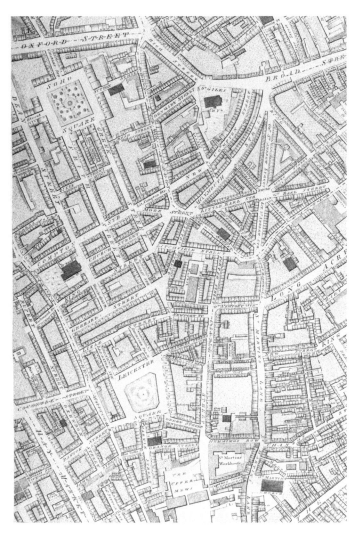

Detail of a plate from Richard Horwood's *Plan of the Cities of London and Westminster, the Borough of Southwark, and Parts adjoining Shewing every House*, 1792-99. The lack of Charing Cross Road is perhaps the most immediately obvious difference between the seventeenth-century map and the Soho streets of today. Charing Cross Road was opened in 1887.

Chapter 2 **The Streets and Squares of Soho**

One of the most striking features of the history of Soho is the spectacular growth and subsequent decline of the many Soho communities, which this chapter reveals by exploring some of the most famous and notorious streets of the area. Soho's streets tell the fascinating story of the area's evolution from a fairly isolated part of London, dominated by manufacturing and poverty, to one of the most iconic cultural hubs in London. Naturally the history of Soho's squares – in this instance Soho Square and Leicester Square – and their importance for Soho's residents, as well as the cultural and commercial life of the area, are also a vital part of this story.

The streets and squares of Soho, some of them among the most famous in the world, are steeped in history, having been home to famous Londoners throughout the centuries and host to a broad range of establishments ranging from embassies and mansions to ballrooms, theatres, restaurants, bars, workshops, nightclubs and brothels. In addition, unlike today, for much of its past the area was also shrouded in an aura of mystery. As temperance reformer Arthur Sherwell observed in 1901, 'so far as the more intimate facts of its moral and social life are concerned, Soho remains to a very large extent a *terra incognita* to the outsider'.[1]

Although Soho during the nineteenth and twentieth centuries was a magnet for famous artists and writers, as well as those less salubrious characters associated with prostitution and vice, many of the district's residents were in fact ordinary and often poor working-class Londoners, living in tight-knit communities from highly diverse immigrant backgrounds. Soho's cosmopolitan population was mostly made up of Austrians, French, Germans, Greeks, Hungarians, Irish, Italians, Spaniards and Swiss. Then, in the latter half of the nineteenth century, Jewish immigrants flocked to Soho in search of refuge and a better life. Chinese immigrants were to continue this trend and add to the international flavour of the area in the second half of the twentieth century. Although estimates varied considerably, by the end of the nineteenth century the vicar of St Anne's church in Dean Street thought that as many as two-thirds of the 12,000 members of his parish were from overseas. Count Armfelt observed, in 1903, that 'no part of the world presents in such a small area so many singular and interesting pictures of cosmopolitan life as Soho'.[2]

A closer look at Soho's thoroughfares also reveals that by no means all observers welcomed the cosmopolitan character of Soho that was emerging around the turn of the last century, and some regarded the 'vast horde of foreign scoundrels who nightly assemble in certain low cafes in Soho' as a constant 'source of much trouble to the police and the public'.[3] Hostility towards the cosmopolitan nature of the district was frequently voiced in the press, with one paper commenting in 1896 that the population of Soho spoke 'a sort of mongrel, bestial dialect, more fit for the lips of gorillas and chimpanzees . . . a sort of reeking hotch-potch of obscene, and often quite meaningless expression'.[4]

The population of the district was furthermore characterised by its proximity to the wealthy residents of Mayfair and St James's on the other side of Regent Street. This grand thoroughfare had been designed by John Nash, in the early nineteenth century, as both a ceremonial route and to establish a 'complete separation between the Streets and Squares occupied by the Nobility and Gentry, and the narrower Streets and meaner houses occupied

The aftermath of a street brawl between immigrants in Soho. Illustration by Gilbert Holiday, published in *The Graphic*, 1911. The original caption commented that, although many of the foreigners in Soho were hard-working craftsmen, there was also an idle element who caused trouble.

by mechanics and the trading part of the community'.[5] This area, stretching from Regent Street to Charing Cross Road, although small in size, housed 24,000 people by 1901. It was here that, 'hidden from all the glare and the glitter are the poor who live by ministering the luxuries of others'.[6]

Soho's communities, despite their close proximity to each other and although generally coexisting in harmony, were in fact largely isolated from each other. A Jewish resident of inter-war Soho remembered that 'we didn't know the French and the Italians, because they were in Frith Street, Greek Street and Dean Street, and we never went there. What did we need to go there for when we had everything we needed where we were?' Alongside the many tales of close-knit communities, a journey through Soho's past also reveals that anonymity was a very common feature. In a description of Soho in the late 1930s, the novelist Gerald Kersh wrote: 'I said, he lived in a room next to mine. But in London you may live and die in a room, and the man next door may never know.'[7]

The famous busker Henry Hollis, who formed the Road Stars with his brother Albert in 1952, remembered the darker side of Soho's streets of the 1950s and 1960s:

> Behind the bright lights and glamour of the West End there is a side the tourist never sees. There is the filth and the garbage you would never dream of. They say that if you stand in Piccadilly long enough you will see every nationality under the sun go by. To see the West End with its glamour stripped off you must go round the back streets in the middle of the night, long after the spivs and prostitutes have gone to bed.[8]

In many respects Hollis's descriptions also fit the Soho of the 1850 and, despite the increasingly gentrified appearance of Soho's streets, traces of this darker side of the district are still evident to this day.

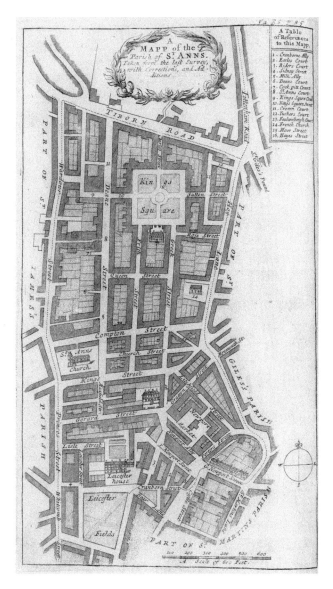

Map of the parish of St Anne, in John Stow, *A Survey of the Cities of London and Westminster: Containing the Original, Antiquity, Increase, Modern Estate and Government of those Cities*. Revised edition by John Strype, 1720.

Although in the seventeenth and eighteenth centuries many of the thoroughfares of the area were designed to be inhabited by London's wealthy elites, as early as the mid-nineteenth century the character of the area had changed significantly. A stark portrayal of this change in popular culture was provided by R. L. Stevenson's famous novel *Strange Case of Doctor Jekyll and Mr Hyde*, written in 1886, in which Hyde's home was located in 'the dismal quarter of Soho . . . with its muddy ways and slatternly passengers'.

Our tour through the history of Soho's thoroughfares begins in the eastern part of the district, which was established as the parish of St Anne in the late seventeenth century and is where the name of the area originated. Here Henry VIII had acquired hunting fields during the dissolution of the monasteries, which most likely explains the connection with the Anglo-French hunting call, 'Soho!' The area west of present-day Wardour Street, built in a more haphazard manner and often housing poorer residents, was not originally part of Soho but rather of the parish of St James. It was only 'annexed' to Soho after the building of Regent Street in the 1820s, and some distinctions between the two parts persisted throughout their history. The east tended to be more prosperous, while the busy streets of St James's attracted the poorer trades and also became the major West End location for Jewish tailors.

Dean Street

A fascinating example that highlights the changing fortunes and transformation of Soho is Dean Street. Built in the 1680s, it is one of the longest streets in the district, crossing nearly all of Soho from Oxford Street in the north to Shaftesbury Avenue and what is now the area known as Chinatown. It was home to several titled inhabitants in its early seventeenth-century days. By the eighteenth century a number of artists had moved in, including John Francis Rigaud, Francis Hayman and William

Beechey (best known for his 1791 painting of Lord Nelson), and in 1895 historian E. F. Rimbault was writing that Soho was renowned for 'the very large number of eminent characters [who] resided here at various times'.[9] He includes mention of No. 17 Dean Street – once housing the library of the botanist Joseph Banks, it was to be the home of Robert Brown, the keeper of the Botanical Department of the British Museum, for over thirty years until his death in 1858. Towards the end of the century craftsmen began to take over a number of houses, while other residences were turned into restaurants.

One of the most famous residents of Dean Street was the revolutionary thinker Karl Marx. After the failed liberal 1848 revolution in Prussia he fled to London. Having been evicted from the German Hotel in Lisle Street, due to not being able to pay his bill, he and his family moved to two small rooms at 28 Dean Street, where they lived for five years (from 1850 to 1856). His perilous financial situation and the cramped and insanitary living conditions undoubtedly contributed to the death of two of his young children during his stay in Soho, and his long-suffering wife Jenny was reduced to begging £2 from a neighbour to pay for one of the children's coffins.

It was the arrival of political refugees like Marx that made Soho increasingly notorious for its radical clubs and newfound status of 'refuge for dangerous cosmopolitanism'.[10] When the news of the 1848 revolution in France arrived in Britain, London's 'Frenchmen, Germans, Poles, Magyars, sprang to their feet, embraced, shouted, and gesticulated in the wildest enthusiasm ... [they then] marched to the meeting-place of the Westminster Chartists, in Dean Street, Soho. There another enthusiastic fraternisation took place, and great was the clinking of glasses that night in and around Soho and Leicester Square'.[11] Unsurprisingly the press had a field day when Martial Bourdin, a Soho lady's tailor and anarchist of French descent, was killed when a bomb he carried exploded prematurely near the Greenwich Observatory in 1894.

Programme cover for performance of *Trial by Jury* at the Royalty Theatre, 1875.

The reputation of the area sank so low that, in 1900, *Cassell's Saturday Journal* confidently claimed that Soho was a haven for many foreign anarchists who 'meet at regular intervals to discuss the most diabolical plots of revenge on society'.[12]

Dean Street also had early associations with London's entertainment industries. No. 73 housed the Royalty Theatre, a small and obscure space built in 1834–37 at the rear of the Dean Street also had early associations with London's entertainment industries. No. 73 housed the Royalty Theatre, a small and obscure space built in 1834–37 at the rear of the actress and singer Fanny Kelly's house. Originally known as 'Miss Kelly's Theatre', it was the brainchild of the ageing actress and built under the patronage of the Duke of Devonshire. The opening was delayed by at least three years due to the installation of new, prize-winning stage machinery. Unfortunately this new technology turned the opening night of the theatre into an embarrassing disaster, forcing the venue to close down only a week after its much publicised opening. The machinery was so noisy that it proved impossible to hear the play being performed on the stage. Kelly's health deteriorated due to the resulting public ridicule and financial strain, and in 1849 she was evicted by the landlord, having lost £16,000 on the venture. Prior to her eviction the theatre was briefly used by The Amateurs, the first amateur theatre company in the UK. Featuring among them was one Charles Dickens. He had honoured Kelly by writing a prologue for a production by The Amateurs to be spoken by her.

In 1854 the theatre was reopened by T. H. Mowbray as the Soho Theatre – 'sometimes jocularly known as the "So-so Theatre".'[13] Productions included French plays, performed for the benefit of the large number of French residents in the neighbourhood. Later in the nineteenth century the theatre – now the New Royalty Theatre – became chiefly famous for its French and German pieces. In 1875 Richard D'Oyly Carte produced his first ever Gilbert and Sullivan opera, *Trial by Jury*, at the theatre.

The success of this piece helped to cement the reputation of the Gilbert and Sullivan cooperation. Later performances at the theatre included the 1892 premiere of George Bernard Shaw's *Widower's Houses*; the first London appearance of the Irish National Theatre Society in 1904; and Noël Coward's eleventh play, *The Vortex*, in 1924. The venue nonetheless constantly struggled to compete with its larger and more famous rivals. In 1892 Brandon Thomas's *Charley's Aunt* had been a huge hit for the theatre – and, precisely because of its success, it transferred to the much larger Globe Theatre after only two weeks. The final curtain at the Royalty fell in 1937, when the theatre was closed because of fire risk.

In the twentieth century Dean Street became home to a number of pubs and clubs frequented by Soho's bohemia such as the Golden Lion, a magnet for gay soldiers and sailors passing through war-time London, the French-run Caves de France, and the Colony Room, run by the infamous Muriel Belcher. Dean Street's drinking holes also included the famous York Minster, which had been run by German immigrants until the outbreak of the First World War in 1914. The licence was acquired by Belgian Victor Berlemont, after which the pub became somewhat erroneously known as 'the French pub'. It stayed in the hands of the same family for much of the twentieth century, and was renamed the French House in 1984. The street also houses the Groucho Club at No. 44, previously the site of Soho's first Italian restaurant.

Like many parts of London, Soho's streets were affected by bombing in the Second World War. The physical destruction and social impact on the communities of Soho caused by the Blitz was highly significant for the development of the area in the second half of the twentieth century. Although the most notorious casualty in the area was the Café de Paris in Coventry Street, much of Soho was severely affected by bombing. Carlisle House, an elegant eighteenth-century mansion just off Dean Street, was completely destroyed during the Blitz in May 1941.

CARLISLE HOUSE
17th-Century Sir Christopher Wren Mansion.

KEEBLE (1914) LTD.

10 CARLISLE STREET
SOHO, LONDON, W.

INTERIOR DECORATIONS

ELECTRIC LIGHT
FITTINGS.

ANTIQUE FURNITURE.

REPRODUCTIONS

Advertisement for Keeble Ltd., interior decorators based at Carlisle House, published in G. C. Wilton, *The Story of Soho*, 1925.

'St Anne's, Soho [from a sketch taken in 1840].' Engraving from W. Thornbury, *Old & New London*, Cassell 1898.

In the same month, dozens of people lost their lives when the building housing the famous Patisserie Valerie Restaurant at No. 59 was completely destroyed during a night-time raid. Another prominent victim was the parish church of St Anne, located between Dean and Wardour Streets. Only its imposing clock tower survived the repeated attacks on the site. Although the destruction of the church was a great loss for the local community, the architectural style of the building had proved to be controversial in the past:

> The singularly shaped spire of St Anne's has earned for this build-ing the reputation of being one of the ugliest churches in London. This extraordinary spire, although the most prominent, is not the only unsightly feature in the fabric, and it seems not a little curi-ous that St Anne's Parish, which was formed out of a portion of that of St Martin-in-the-Fields, should have a church of such mean and inadequate character, whilst its mother-church, in Trafalgar Square, is such a well-known and universally admired example of ecclesiastical architecture. Yet, St Anne's Church was designed by Sir Christopher Wren.[14]

So rich is the history of Dean Street that an individual house can provide fascinating insight into the lives of the people of Soho throughout the centuries. Such is the case with No. 21, which in its early days was the site of the Venetian Ambassador's chapel. From 1748 to 1763 it was Caldwell's Assembly Rooms. Here Mozart, aged seven, played the harpsichord accompanied by his four-year-old sister in 1763. The building was later a dancing academy, auction room and warehouse and, from 1872 to 1939, it was St Anne's National School. In 1944 it became the West End Street Synagogue, rebuilt in 1961–63 to include an art gallery, before finally being converted in 1999–2000 into premises for the Soho Theatre. The history of this single house strikingly illuminates the complexity of Soho's historic connections with religion, the arts and entertainment, as well as the cosmopolitan nature of the district.

Dean Street in the 1920s. Photograph by Lasky Film Service Ltd., published in G. C. Wilton, *The Story of Soho*, 1925.

Gerrard Street

At the southern end of Dean Street lies Gerrard Street, the present-day heart of Soho's Chinatown. However, the reputation of Gerrard Street as a multicultural centre predates the emergence of Chinatown by centuries. There had been three waves of French immigration into Soho, and Gerrard Street served as a key destination for each of them. The first occurred in 1685 when a large number of Huguenots fled after the Revocation of the Edict of Nantes. The second wave came during the French Revolution, and the third wave brought French communists to Soho in 1871.

Soho was increasingly becoming a centre for French religious and charitable institutions. The nineteenth century saw the establishment of the French Hospital and Dispensary in Shaftesbury Avenue (in 1867), the French schools in Lisle Street (in 1865) and the Catholic L'Eglise de Notre Dame de France church, located just off Leicester Square (in 1868). But it was the establishment of coffee houses and restaurants around Gerrard Street that helped to establish Soho's reputation as London's equivalent to the Quartier Latin in Paris, with its café culture, during the nineteenth century.

As the age of revolution progressed on the continent, it brought ever new waves of immigrants to Soho, such as Italians and Germans in the 1860s and 1870s. They further added to the 'culinary explosion' that centred on Gerrard Street at the end of the nineteenth century, while an air of political intrigue was being created by writers, artists and those generally at odds with the establishment, who had begun to colonise the street and its surrounding area. The Mont Blanc Restaurant at No. 16 was favoured by writers such as Belloc, Chesterton, Galsworthy and Ford Madox Ford. It was at No. 4 that Virginia Woolf's husband Leonard and some of his friends founded the 1917 Club, a socialist establishment where intellectuals, political activists, artists and writers congregated until its demise in the early 1930s.

BOULOGNE RESTAURANT, 27 GERRARD STREET, LONDON, W.1

Managing Proprietors: A. SPIRITI. G. MAGGI.

Withïn 3 minutes of all West End Theatres and places of Amusement

· ·

Telephone:
GERRARD
3186

Banqueting Rooms for Weddings, Masonic and Regimental Dinners.

— · ·

Telephone:
GERRARD
3186

Postcard advertising Boulogne Restaurant at 27 Gerrard Street, 1936.

By the 1930s the area resembled 'a little state of Italy joined to a fragment of one of the more distant of the French *departements*'.[15] American jazz entered the fold in the inter-war period with Kate Meyrick's 43 Club hosting bands such as the famous ones led by Paul Whiteman, Paul Specht and Hal Kemp in the early 1920s. The Big Apple in Gerrard Street catered especially for black men in the 1930s.

Although Chinese restaurants were already established in the area by the inter-war period, the emergence of Chinatown around Gerrard and Lisle Street only occurred during the 1950s. Prior to this, London's Chinatown was located in the East End, mostly in Limehouse. It was the communist takeover in China in 1949 that led to an influx of Chinese refugees into war-scarred Soho. They quickly established restaurants that were increasingly popular with theatregoers, students looking for a cheap meal, and former British servicemen who had acquired a taste for Chinese food when serving in Asia. By the middle of the 1960s Gerrard Street was known in Cantonese as *Tong Yahn* or 'Chinese People's Street'. Chinese immigrants, often speaking very few words of English and armed with the intention of going back home soon after having sent some money to the families they left behind, referred to Soho as 'the Imperial City'.[16]

Old Compton Street

Running parallel to the north of Gerrard Street and Shaftesbury Avenue, as well as crossing Dean Street, is Old Compton Street. From its earliest days it possessed special interest in the history of Soho, and demands something more than a mere passing note of its inhabitants at different times, varied as they were in station and character. John Strype, in his 1720 survey of London said, 'Compton Street, very long . . . is broad, and the houses well built, but of no great account for its inhabitants, which are chiefly French'.[17]

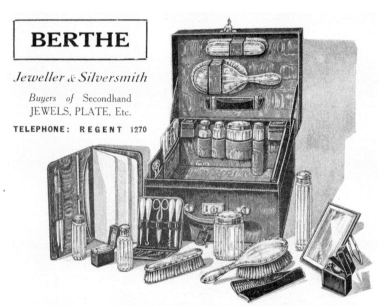

BERTHE

Jeweller & Silversmith

Buyers of Secondhand
JEWELS, PLATE, Etc.

TELEPHONE: REGENT 1270

40 OLD COMPTON STREET, SOHO, W.

Advertisement for Berthe jewellers and silversmiths of 40 Old Compton Street, published in
G. C. Wilton, *The Story of Soho*, 1925.

From its beginnings Old Compton Street was one of Soho's main shopping streets, and many of its residents were foreign. The French poets Verlaine and Rimbaud gave readings at their favourite bar in the street and, particularly after the suppression of the Paris Commune in 1871, it became a recognised meeting place for French exiles. By the mid-nineteenth century nearly all the houses in the street were used as shops. Old Compton Street was considered to be 'as French as the rue St Honoré' as late as the 1930s, and it was dominated by French businesses. One shop devoted itself entirely to the sale of snails and frogs. An observer noticed in 1905 that 'in the window is a two-storied doll's house constructed entirely of snails' shells; live snails cling to the window-panes'.[18]

By the 1950s the street was chiefly famous for its coffee bars, such as the Amalfi, Prego Bar Restaurant and, most famously, the 2i's Coffee Bar at No. 59. Run by two Australians from 1955, it was named after the original proprietors, the brothers Freddie and Sammy Irani. With a tiny stage in the basement it was to play a major role in the emergence of British pop music in the late 1950s. It is during this period that Old Compton Street began to acquire its reputation as the 'epitome of hard-core hedonism'.[19]

Frith Street and Greek Street

Crossing Old Compton Street and running parallel to Dean Street are Frith Street and Greek Street. In the eighteenth century the young Mozart, during the London part of a European tour organised by his father, stayed at No. 21 Frith Street. The street underwent a similar transformation to that of Dean Street, seeing its aristocratic residents increasingly replaced by artisans, artists and writers by the early nineteenth century, and later tradesmen and craftsmen moved in, joined by restaurant keepers. John Logie Baird lived at No. 22 from 1924 to 1926 where, in his attic room, he gave the first public demonstration of television to members of the Royal

'Greek Street, "the foreign quarter of London", called "the worst street in London" by an Inspector McKay, giving evidence before the Police Commission. 1. Soho types. 2. A corner in Greek Street. 3. A popular club. 4. A fortune teller. 5. A musical evening'. Drawing by L. Daviel, *Illustrated London News*, 27 October 1906. This edition of the *Illustrated London News* describes Greek Street as a 'haunt of choice rascaldom'.

Institution. By the early 1950s Soho had begun to transform into the cultural phenomenon we know today, with the introduction of Italian-style coffee bars. The first Gaggia espresso machine came to Frith Street in 1953, launching the vogue for Italian coffee, food and fashion. The Mika coffee bar was the first of many to 'acquire a powerful mystique as [an oasis] of alternative culture in London'.[20]

To the east of Frith Street, Greek Street achieved notoriety in 1906 when a Metropolitan Police Inspector publicly declared that it was 'the worst street in the West End of London' and that 'crowds of people gather there nightly who are little else than a pest. I will go further and say that some of the vilest reptiles in London live there or frequent it'.[21] Although the charge was categorically denied by the vicar at St Anne's, the national press nonetheless carried the headlines of 'the worst street in London' in the days to follow. It is worth pointing out that, prior to this controversy, the Metropolitan Police itself had been charged with corruption and bribery in regards to prostitution, gambling and the ill treatment of foreigners.

On the corner of Greek Street and Romilly Street, the French Restaurant Kettner's was founded in 1868. It was Oscar Wilde's favourite London eatery, and some of Soho's rent boys were wined and dined by him here before being taken to nearby hotels for sex. By the beginning of the twentieth century Greek Street was famous for its brothels, while some of the restaurants and 'hotels' across Soho also offered rooms for sexual services to their customers.

Berwick Street and Broadwick Street

Having examined the eastern areas of Soho it is now time to cross Wardour Street, the seventeenth-century western border of Soho, into Berwick Street and Broadwick Street. Berwick Street is most famous for its street market. One of the oldest in London, it dates back to the eighteenth century when traders began to display their wares on the pavement, but it was only officially recognised as a market in 1892. It is believed it was probably here that a market trader introduced the grapefruit to Londoners. The hustling and bustling of Berwick Street Market left such an impression on Virginia Woolf in the 1920s that she used it in her fiction; she also took pride in her ability to haggle with the stall keepers and the shop touts (known as 'schleppers').

In the mid-nineteenth century Berwick Street had been in the centre of a densely crowded area of slum buildings, and many of the residents had succumbed to the 1854 outbreak of cholera. An example of a much more recent architecture in the street is Kemp House, designed by L. C. Holbrook. The seventeen-storey block of council flats, built in the 1960s, serves as a brutal reminder of what might have become of Soho had the comprehensive redevelopment plans that were drawn up after 1945 been fully realised. Kemp House was home to the famous columnist and alcoholic Jeffrey Bernard. Bernard wrote for both the *New Statesman* and the *Spectator*, but his alcoholism led to regular notifications to the readers of his columns that 'Jeffrey Bernard is unwell'. This was the title of the successful 1989 West End play by Keith Waterhouse, starring Peter O'Toole. Bernard, having been warned as early as 1965 that he might well die if he touched another drink, lived another thirty-two years before succumbing to kidney failure. The famous cover photograph of the 1995 Oasis album *(What's the Story) Morning Glory?* was taken in Berwick Street, which was at this time still host to many specialist outlets for recorded music.

The Blue Posts pub, at the junction with Broadwick Street, has been on the same site since at least 1739. Broadwick Street was given its name in 1936 when Broad Street and Edward Street were joined. The John Snow pub on the corner of Lexington Street was named after Dr John Snow in 1956, to commemorate his decision to have the handle of the nearby water pump chained up during the 1854 cholera outbreak. He was convinced the disease was not caused by 'bad air', but rather

'Berwick Street on a Sunday Morning.' Plate in G. R. Sims [ed.], *Living London. Its Work and its Play. Its Humour and its Pathos. Its Sights and its Scenes*, Cassell 1901.

waterborne. The inhabitants of only twelve out of the forty-nine houses survived the epidemic. The survivors, all working in the local brewery, were drinking beer instead of water. His findings contributed to fundamental changes in London's water supply.

Carnaby Street

At the end of Broadwick Street, and close to Soho's western border, lies Carnaby Street, one of London's most famous thoroughfares. Taking its name from Karnaby House, a mansion previously standing on its site, Carnaby Street in the nineteenth century contributed to Soho's notoriety as a breeding ground for revolutionary political activity. It is said that at the Nag's Head pub the provocative toast was: 'May the last of the kings be strangled with the guts of the last of the priests'.[22]

It was the youth revolution of the 1960s that transformed Carnaby Street from a dreary backwater filled with small clothes factories into the most famous shopping street in Britain. The transformation was largely due to the Scottish clothing entrepreneur John Stephen, founder of menswear shops that were aimed at a new clientele who wanted colour and pattern rather than the traditional grey suit. When a fire damaged the premises of his shop His Clothes on Beak Street, Stephen opened a new shop at No. 41 Carnaby Street. Partly due to new marketing ideas, such as experimental window displays and racks on the pavements, it proved so successful that by the middle of the decade Stephen owned around a third of the shops in Carnaby Street, each sporting a variation of his name, such as Stephen John's Man Shop.

However, despite this success, the American journalist Piri Halasz, author of the famous 1966 *Time* article on Swinging London, seemed unimpressed. She warned in her *A Swinger's Guide to London* that 'the kind of clothes you probably are interested in buying are *not* in the Carnaby Street shops . . . You

Advertisement for the John Stephen shops on Carnaby Street, published in *London Life*, 1966.

will find better, finer clothes in the small boutiques in Chelsea and Mayfair . . . Don't forget that mass pop fashion in Britain . . . is apt to be cheaply made and the fabrics sometimes shoddy.' She went on to comment: 'On Carnaby Street is Lady Jane, with noisy pop music and many designers. The smaller Tre Camp is owned by John Stephen, and has dressing rooms papered with six-foot-tall pictures of men in bathing trunks.'[23]

Great Windmill Street

To the south-west of the district, and equally as renowned as Carnaby Street for creating Soho's colourful reputation, is Great Windmill Street, named after a seventeenth-century windmill. In the early 1850s Karl Marx gave a series of lectures above the Red Lion pub. It was in this street, too, that Robert Bignell opened the Argyll Assembly Rooms, which quickly became a popular haunt for prostitutes and their clients. Perhaps most famous, however was the Windmill Theatre, which entertained and shocked London audiences with its displays of nudity for thirty-two years before finally closing its doors in 1964.

On the corner of Windmill Street and Archer Street, Club 11 opened as one of the first jazz basement clubs of 1950s London. Run by jazz musicians Ronnie Scott and John Dankworth, it became the driving force for a newly emerging underground culture that was defined by music, rather than literature as in the 1930s. Due to the popularity of marijuana among its customers, it was closed down by the police. Reopened as Cy Laurie's Jazz Club, the venue hosted one of London's first all-night jazz sessions in 1951, a very novel and exciting concept, organised among others by the singer George Melly. Today, Great Windmill Street continues to house Soho Parish School, the only school in Soho since the 1820s.

Valerie, a member of the Revudeville Company, in her dressing room at the Windmill Theatre. Photograph by Tunbridge-Sedgwick for the *Bystander*, 30 October 1940.

Created in the 1880s at the southern end of Great Windmill Street, these major new thoroughfares cut through the King Street and New Market slums and turned Soho into the centre of London's Theatreland. Six theatres were built on Shaftesbury Avenue alone, although in 1927 one writer considered it 'a nondescript roadway lacking vistas . . . a story of wasted opportunity . . . a street where pedestrians "hurry by"'.[24] The same was arguably true for Charing Cross Road, which meets Shaftesbury Avenue at Cambridge Circus. It had long been felt that a street linking Tottenham Court Road and Charing Cross was needed. In order to create the new road, a significant number of existing streets were either modified or absorbed, including Crown Street, Moor Street, Grafton Street, Lichfield Street, Porter Street and Castle Street, along with other minor streets and courts.

Opened in 1887, Charing Cross Road established the eastern boundary of present-day Soho but, due to the unwillingness of the Metropolitan Board of Works to provide more funding, was rather less grand and distinguished than Regent Street. As cultural historian Judith Walkowitz notes, 'It retained all the "pot-houses" of old Crown Street, while over time accruing a miscellaneous collection of theatres, dark, brooding tenements, second-hand book-stores, "rubber good stores", pornography shops, and government offices towards its southern end.'[25] Although itself not very impressive, the street nonetheless had a significant impact on Soho.

Soho Square

Lying just to the west of Charing Cross Road's northern end, Soho Square amply demonstrates – albeit on a small scale – the main changes that affected all of Soho, and indeed serves as a fascinating example of the complete transformation of central

Monmouth House, Soho Square. Engraving from W. Thornbury, *Old & New London*, 1898. Built for the Duke of Monmouth in the 1680s, the mansion was bought in 1716 by Sir James Bateman. It was leased to high-profile figures such as Count de Guerchy, the French ambassador. In 1773 the Bateman family decided it would be demolished, with a number of buildings for leasehold built in its place. These comprised two large houses (Nos 28 and 29 Soho Square), with several smaller dwellings behind.

London over the centuries. After its illustrious beginnings in the late seventeenth century, its fortunes changed. Like most parts of Soho suffering from the early Victorian decline into poverty, the relative isolation of the square from wide streets, and the dubious character of the surrounding narrow streets, had been a distinct disadvantage to businesses. In 1882 a vestry of the parish report stated that the neighbourhood of Soho Square was 'a veritable focus of every danger which can menace the health and social order of a city. The houses, from their insanitary conditions, are horribly disgusting, and can only be fitly designated as [a] well-prepared propagating ground for every kind of contagious and loathsome disease . . . The grossest immorality flourishes unabashed from every age downwards to mere children'.[26]

With the opening of Shaftesbury Avenue and Charing Cross Road in 1886, however, many of these undesirable buildings were removed. Writing in the 1940s, Margaret Goldsmith commented: 'Soho was no longer a quiet spot on the map of London . . . The centuries of the square's topographical privacy were over.'[27]

An earlier attempt to overcome the isolation of the square had been made by the businessman Mr W. G. Nixey of No. 12 Soho Square, who in the 1850s found a novel way to advertise his products and draw customers into his premises:

Seldom have modern advertisements surpassed in boldness of idea and success in its result the famous device which may be said to have founded the firm of Mr. W. G. Nixey's Black Lead . . . This representative of Mr Nixey's was dressed in complete armour, well-polished with the new black lead. He was mounted on a magnificent black charger, also in a coat of mail, and carried a banner, on which was the then strange device: W.G. Nixey's Refined Black Lead. His stately progress through the streets of London was attended by enormous crowds and . . . caused such excitement and obstruction that Parliament was petitioned to prohibit such unheard-of novelties.[28]

In less than fifty years the character of the square changed completely. On the occasion of the 1893 St Anne's church bazaar in Soho Square, the *Daily News* reported that 'the square, which has historical associations not excelled by any other spot in London, had . . . been turned into a pleasant summer garden . . . It was more easy than under normal conditions to believe that Soho Square in the earlier part of the century had been one of the most fashionable and rural districts of London'.[29]

In 1938 the original statue of Charles II, carved for the square in 1681 by Danish sculptor Caius Gabriel Cibber but removed during the nineteenth century, was restored to its central location in the square, where it still stands today.

Leicester Square

Equally impressive, if quite different, was the transformation of Leicester Square. The square had been in decline at the beginning of the nineteenth century, and by the mid-century it was being described as one of the most neglected spots in London. Shortly thereafter, however, it became the site for many famous exhibitions and shows: 'Besides the Great Globe and Miss Linwood's Exhibition, there were the Panopticon, Burford's Panorama, and the Eidophusikon in Lisle Street; and . . . numerous entertainments of all kinds provided by . . . Daly's Theatre, the Panopticum, and other neighbouring establishments'.[30]

In fact, towards the end of the nineteenth century, Leicester Square underwent a complete makeover, which turned it into the most important entertainment hub on Soho's southern border. The road expansion to Coventry Street, the renovation of the central gardens, and the construction of elite variety theatres such as the Alhambra and the Empire turned Leicester Square into what has been described as 'the spectacular front stage of the West End pleasure zone'.[31] The area now offered a range of entertainments devoted to the exhibition of the female form.

Leicester Square. Photograph by Alvin Langdon Coburn, 1909.

By the late nineteenth century the square had become the most popular place in London, attracting overseas and provincial visitors with its world-wide reputation for naughtiness. During the 'naughty nineties' Leicester Square's theatres were at the epicentre of West End immorality, with its prostitutes, drinking dens, variety theatres, supper clubs, dancing and gambling halls.

The Wider Picture

Leicester Square's transformation in many respects reflects the changes in all of Soho. The poverty of the area did not completely disappear, but it was increasingly masked by the economic, cultural and social changes that turned Soho into one of the main centres of London's entertainment. From the late nineteenth century onwards, the increasing availability and affordability of public transport, restaurants, theatres, cinemas and cafés, together with newly emerging retail outlets, brought to the area an ever-increasing number of visitors.

This brief whirlwind tour through the streets and squares of Soho provides just a small glimpse into the lives of some of the people of the area, and how some of its most famous and notorious places were affected by its transformation. The rapidly changing character of Soho, its transformation from a poverty-stricken and overcrowded slum in the mid-nineteenth century to London's premier entertainment hub of the 1950s, can be understood by visiting the history of Soho's streets, squares and houses. But in order to really grasp the changes affecting Soho, a look at its inhabitants and its visitors is required. The next chapter sheds some light on how Sohoites made a living, and how the businesses that gave the area its character changed over the years.

Shop-bill, believed to have been designed after Hogarth, for Ellis Gamble, goldsmith, in Cranbourn Street, Leicester Fields. Engraving in W. Thornbury, *Old & New London*, 1898.

Chapter 3   **Making a Living**

By the beginning of the twentieth century it had become increasingly evident that, over the course of every day, Soho underwent a magical transformation 'from a grubby, foreign daytime scene'[1] to a night-time hub taken over by metropolitan revellers who brought an air of success to the area. Soho's day-time and night-time economies, often contrasting in their nature, nevertheless tended to blend into one another and thereby combined to make a vital contribution to the unique character of the area. The stalls of Berwick Street Market stayed open late into the evening, attracting housewives, businesswomen and local prostitutes alike, while the nude performances at the Windmill Theatre began in the early afternoon.

No exploration of Soho's history would be complete without considering both daytime and night-time Soho, and the attempts of its people to get by. Like no other part of London, the businesses, trades, markets, restaurants, nightclubs and gambling dens of Soho attracted London's rich and poor, tourists, shoppers, businessmen and those seeking pleasures of the kind Soho was famed for. It is the way the people of Soho have made a living – whether in poverty or luxury – and how this has changed through the years, which this chapter highlights. It is partly the nature of Soho's commerce that led the area to become a place where, as historian Judith Walkowitz describes it, 'Jews and Gentiles, foreigners and English people, gangsters and bohemians, chorus girls and suburban matrons, interacted with female clerical workers and factory girls'.[2] Although the division is crude, the story of Soho by day features separately, so as to highlight the contrast to the hub of cosmopolitan leisure and London's underworld that is Soho by night.

Soho by Day

Harry Jones, the vicar of St Luke's Berwick Street, commented in 1866 that the area was 'crammed with artisans of all kinds' and that there were 'seamstresses, diamond cutters, sweeps, pianofortes, jewellers, artificial teeth men, pearlstringers, bookbinders, printers and sausage makers'.[3] By the late nineteenth century a vast array of different industries had settled in Soho, ranging from food production, silversmiths, clockmakers, saddlers and carpenters to musical-instrument makers and booksellers: 'If anybody wants the richest of books for ninepence, or a piece of old ware full of bearded figures, which he does not know whether he should give twopence for, or two guineas, this is the place to look for it.'[4]

Some of Soho's trades were quite unusual. The sale of human hair is recorded as a major business (the convents of France, Spain and Italy supplied dark hair, whereas fair hair came from Germany, Austria, Hungary and Alsace-Lorraine). Wardour Street in particular had become famous for the surreal mix of goods on offer, ranging from 'the pseudo-archaic diction affected by modern novelists to a perfectly modern article with a sham appearance of the real antique about it', as one dictionary put it.[5] Apparently the annual destruction of 1,140 elephants was required to satisfy the growing demand for the ivory billiard balls manufactured by Burroughes & Watts of Soho Square, who also introduced India-rubber cushions, leather cue-tips and slate beds to London.

Although Soho's artist communities had moved away to Fitzroy Square, St John's Wood and Chelsea by the late nineteenth century, Newman Street in Soho remained a centre for artists' colour-men (companies manufacturing and supplying artist's materials). On Sundays waiters from the Italian restaurants of

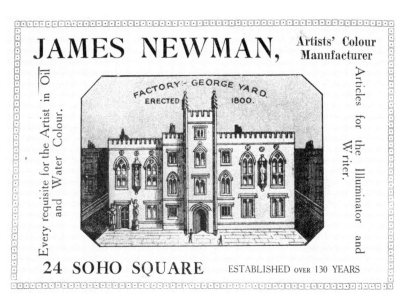

Advertisement for James Newman, artists' colour manufacturer, at 24 Soho Square, published in G. C. Wilton, *The Story of Soho*, 1925.

the area tried to make some extra money by selling watches, bracelets and other trinkets left behind by their customers. The rag trade, which was to make Carnaby Street world famous in the 1960s, was also long established in the area. There were some seventy tailors in the Golden Square area by the First World War. Carnaby Street's connection with the industry had humble beginnings in the 1950s, with the small terraced houses having attic workshops that were cheap to rent.

Soho's economy was shaped by the changes in the immediate surroundings. The building of Regent Street in the 1820s firmly established Soho's western boundaries, and isolated the area from the wealthy residential areas of the West End. Subsequently the western areas of Soho were turned into an industrial hinterland for the tailors and retailers of Savile Row and Regent Street. This development was confounded by the arrival of Jewish tailors in the area around Berwick Street in the late nineteenth century. The subsequent transformation of Oxford Street on Soho's northern border further increased the tendency to turn much of the area into small backstreet workshops and dormitories designed to supply the newly arrived grand department stores. Much of Soho's seventeenth-century grandeur had therefore well and truly disappeared by the beginning of the twentieth century, and the nature of the area's businesses contributed to the emergence of a district marred by poverty and overcrowding.

Towards the end of the nineteenth century the temperance reformer Arthur Sherwell identified a number of structural weaknesses in Soho's industrial economy. The expansion of the dynamic leisure and retail industries surrounding the area led to an increase of warehouses and workshops in Soho itself, which in turn led to a decline of housing stock and an increase in rent. This then caused Soho to have the highest percentage of families living in one-room tenements in all of London. Furthermore, due to the diversity of different trades and the lack of one dominant industry, the district did not have a specific industrial identity.

'Interior of House in Court'. Illustration by John Brown of a single-room dwelling in Berwick Street, in George Godwin, *London Shadows: A Glance at the 'Homes' of the Thousands*, G. Routledge, 1854.

Many of Soho's industries, such as the provision of food and the production of clothing, were dominated by sweated female labour, further heightening the precarious nature of employment and the prevalence of poverty in the area. Sherwell observed that, at the turn of the century, Soho contained 'all the ordinary facts of social life in crowded centres – insanitary dwellings, irregular employment, sweated wages and chronic physical weakness, intensified by higher rents and a relatively higher cost of living'. All of this was made worse by 'the close proximity of those awful contrasts – the extremes of wealth and poverty, which are the special and peculiar miseries of the West End'.[6] But this was not a new phenomenon. Exactly forty years before Sherwell was writing, John Hollingshead, in his book *Ragged London in 1861*, had explained that it was increasingly common in Soho that 'houses built for a well-to-do class had been deserted by their original tenants, and then filled from cellar to garret by families of artisans compelled to live near their work in Regent Street'.[7]

Despite the problems of poverty and housing, Soho's economy continued to thrive, aided by the transformation of the West End into London's prime retail centre. When Oxford Circus Underground station opened in 1900, at the same time as omnibus services to Oxford Street were improving, West End stores became more accessible to a wider section of society. Sales of ladies' clothing significantly increased. Mantles (loose-fitting outer garments similar to a cape) began to be made in small-scale factories both north and south of Oxford Street, and the wholesale manufacturing of dresses, coats and suits became big business.

Shopping and retail had long been an integral part of day-time Soho. Its reputation as a shopping district had been established during the early nineteenth century with the infamous Soho Bazaar, opened by John Trotter in 1816 to assist war widows whose husbands had died in the Napoleonic Wars. Trotter had lived in Soho Square since 1785, and had

Bazaar, Soho Square. Drawn and published by Henry Perry, 1819.

bought up the entire north-west corner site from No. 4 to No. 7 as he made a fortune selling supplies to the British army. The Bazaar enabled women to sell merchandise at its stalls, thereby encouraging, as E. F. Rimbault expressed it in 1895, 'female and domestic industry'. As the first establishment of its kind in the UK, it proved such a success that only a few months after its opening the average number of visitors per day was 2,500. Rimbault continued: 'Persons of consequence and position made their purchases here in such numbers that the adjacent portions of Soho Square were occupied by two or three rows of waiting carriages.'[8]

Goods sold at the Soho Bazaar mostly comprised jewellery, millinery, gloves, lace and potted plants – and all were produced in the UK. The bazaar was still operating some eighty years later, but by the 1890s its premises had almost entirely been taken over by the publishing company, A. & C. Black. The latter were to remain in Soho Square until 2009 (having been bought by Bloomsbury Publishing in 2000, who occupied the Soho premises at that time).

The Bazaar was far from being the only famous London retail outlet in Soho. Arthur Lasenby Liberty, a draper from Chesham who later became an active member of the Arts and Crafts Society, opened East India House at 218A Regent Street in 1875, selling soft-coloured silks from the East. He extended his range of products to oriental goods of all kinds, including Japanese works and fans. Liberty soon opened two more shops on Regent Street and turned his small business into a large retail emporium and one of London's favourite suppliers of oriental curiosities, fabrics and clothes.

A jeweller's premises that was located between Arthur Liberty's shops had been circumvented by a humped double staircase over its entrance, nicknamed the 'camel's back'. In 1925 the premises were completely rebuilt and replaced by two Liberty buildings. The Great Marlborough Street premises were given a timber façade and a Tudor-style interior made from the

'Liberty Art Fabrics'. Advertisement in G. C. Wilton, *The Story of Soho*, 1925..

remains of two man-o'-war ships, the HMS *Hindustan* and HMS *Impregnable*. Liberty's own stained-glass craftsmen and Italian master carvers lent their skills to the unique building. Liberty's influence on London fashion of the late nineteenth and early twentieth centuries was enormous, and its fame was further enhanced when Gilbert and Sullivan used Liberty's fabrics for some of their costumes.

However, not all of Soho's retail and trading was aimed at wealthy visitors coming into the West End for a day's shopping. During the inter-war period the leisure industries surrounding the area also increasingly attracted working-class customers who, apart from visiting dance halls, cinemas and stores such as Lyons' Corner Houses or Marks & Spencer, also ventured into Soho itself.

This influx of working-class Londoners into Soho caused a transformation of the nature of retail – as expressed by the growth of importance of Berwick Street Market as a shopping destination in its own right. The market had been in existence for two centuries by the time it expanded due to the closure of Monmouth and Newport Markets after Victorian street improvements. Growing from 32 stalls in 1893 to 158 in 1930, the market was increasingly identified with clothing rather than food. Although still dominated by Jewish traders, as in the past, it had now expanded its merchandise to include up-to-date, ready-to-wear fashion, broadening its appeal to a wider audience of all classes.

The changing nature of Berwick Street Market went hand-in-hand with the rise of a new phenomenon after the First World War – the fashion-conscious, young working-class woman, who in the minds of contemporary writers and journalists was 'lipsticked, silk-stockinged, self-confident and looking like an actress'.[9] These energetic young women may have unsettled middle-class Londoners visiting the area, but their arrival undoubtedly led to a new dynamism in the market. Able to present itself as a viable alternative to the rigid class codes and high prices of Oxford Street, Berwick Street Market became popular for much of the inter-war period as a cutting-edge retail space for mass market, ready-to-wear fashion. By the 1920s the market was known as a place where women of all classes could buy all manner of items, from food to fashion.

A travel book on London advised its readers in 1927 that those hunting for bargains could find anything from 'beef to basins' and 'lace to lettuce' on Berwick Street Market, but advised customers to keep their wits about them if they buy goods from 'a foreign-looking stall holder'. The main object of desire, however, was the 'so-called silken hose' that 'twinkles up and down the City streets'.[10] The increasingly aggressive traders sold a whole range of accessories and dancing clothes to shop girls and clerks, many of whom were apparently buying into a prevailing fantasy of leaving the day job and becoming an actress.

The transformation of Berwick Street Market successfully broadened the appeal of Soho to middle-class shoppers, as well as to the many clerical and service workers working in central London who felt that the stores on Oxford Street were too grand and too expensive. Chaim Lewis, whose father owned a shop on Berwick Street, later recalled how impressed he was by the 'transformation almost overnight of a single street of shabby, derelict Georgian terraced houses which was Berwick Street, into an assemblage of chrome and glass-plated shop fronts, each competing for the working-class custom. The pace of development was breathtaking'.[11]

In 1921, journalist Sophie Cole evocatively described Berwick Street Market in her classic volume, *The Lure of Old London*, declaring that the market 'lives out of doors and doesn't wear hats. It takes strangers into its confidence. It thrusts fur coats, frocks and blouses under your nose'.[12] Another of the market's admirers was Virginia Woolf, who wrote in her diary: 'I walked through a narrow street lined on both sides with barrows, where

'Soho: Berwick Market.' Photograph in Paul Cohen-Portheim, *The Spirit of London*, 1935.

stockings, ironmongery, & candles & fish were being sold. A band organ played in the middle. I bought six bundles of coloured tapers. The stir & colour and cheapness [pleased] me to the depths of my soul.'[13]

During this period the market was intimately associated with its aggressive shop touts, known as 'schleppers'. Originally the term had been used to describe Jewish pedlars, a common sight in the London streets of the eighteenth century, labouring under the weight of heavy sacks of soiled, second-hand clothes that they 'schlepped' – meaning to carry something heavy or awkward – through the streets. The 1920s Berwick Street Market schlepper, however, was a rather different character. He had developed into a fast-talking, smartly dressed Jewish shop tout who pressurised customers to come into his store.

Thelma Benjamin explained, in her 1930s guidebook for shopping in London, that outside each shop was a tout, 'and if you stop and look in the window, you will find a hand on your arm and a persuasive voice in your ear, and, unless you are very firm, you will be led into the shop, from which there seems to be no escape except by purchase!'[14] Women shoppers who did not enter the shops were often showered with insults by the schleppers exchanging remarks with each other, such as, 'I'd sooner put a dress on a scarecrow as put it on 'er.' This was 'their charming revenge on you for not visiting their shop when you went by before'.[15] According to one resident of the area, 'they stopped you at the first, the second and the third shop. They wouldn't let you get away. Once they got you in – there was pressure. It provided a marvellous living but then they lost it. They ruined it because the customers did not have a chance to go and look'. Some people felt that the schleppers were responsible for killing off trade. 'People were afraid to look in the windows.'[16]

With the advent of stores on Oxford Street such as Marks & Spencer and others who sold stockings at lower prices than the market traders, Berwick Street Market's fortune declined in the 1930s. The number of police prosecutions of aggressive and overly keen shop touts was increasing, at the same time as the migration of the Jewish community to the suburbs had begun, and both factors combined to hasten the decline of the market. In 1929 virtually all Berwick Street stallholders lived nearby, but by the late 1930s almost half had migrated to suburbs such as Golders Green, lured away by the availability of cheap, modern and affordable suburban housing and the increasingly accessible public transport network. Whereas just after the Great War trade in Berwick Street Market was flourishing, by 1936 it had all gone very quiet. One trader complained that 'Oxford Street has knocked out Berwick Market'.[17]

Wartime rationing, introduced in 1940, further damaged the trade in silk stockings – in 1940 there were ninety-nine businesses along Berwick Street, but only forty-four remained three years later. By 1946 the flood of shoppers had dried up, and the hustle and bustle of market life was gone. According to Stanley Jackson, writing in 1946, 'The two men who seemed to be doing the biggest business were a vendor of cat's meat and a hunchback who was reading horoscopes with the aid of a pencil, a printed list of prophecies and your date of birth.'[18] The flourishing black-market activities in the area dealt the final blow to the reputation of the market, so that by 1946 one of the property owners on Berwick Street went as far as asking Westminster Council to rename the street as they could not find a tenant for their premises. Prior to its revival as a record-shop street, Berwick Street therefore appeared 'rather like a Klondike town after the gold rush'.[19]

Despite the market's demise in the 1940s, Soho increasingly acted as supplier to the entertainment industry, which was growing fast in the immediate surroundings. As the century progressed, Soho was to cater for the working-class customer as much as for the better-off. Sex workers were also an important source of revenue to local traders, as it was often Soho's shop keepers and milliners who supplied them with hats and dresses. Although arguably part of 'night-time Soho', the sex trade was therefore intimately linked to its daytime economy. Berwick Street Market

Shoppers in Berwick Street Market, 16 July 1955. Photograph by Joseph McKeown for *Picture Post – 7855 – London's Little Europe*, 1955.

stockings attracted the street walkers from Lisle Street – 'bold-eyed hussies', who 'traded bawdy jokes with the cockney stall holders'.[20] Many French maids of high-class street walkers (known locally as 'Fifis') were regular customers of the Soho dressmaker mother of Madeleine Mathilde Gal, a French woman who, writing as Mrs Robert Henrey, published several autobiographical works about her life growing up in London in the first half of the twentieth century.[21] A little further down the road many of the shops in Charing Cross Road 'specialise in rejuvenating old men and . . . reckless young women [who] sabotage the stork'.[22]

Soho's broad commercial interests included the publishing industry, which has long been associated particularly with Soho Square. The square's location just off Oxford Street made it an ideal location for businesses, and the publishing house of George Routledge was situated here until 1852. His had been one of the most successful publishing companies at serving the newly emerging readership of the mid-nineteenth century. As reading ceased to be a privilege of the wealthy, publishing was becoming a commercial enterprise. George Routledge was one of the first to understand this, realising that producing cheaper books, aimed at those who wanted to read for pleasure rather than for reference, was the way forward. Routledge's new Railway Library series, issued from Soho Square, served the demands of an ever-increasing number of passengers during the railway boom of the mid-nineteenth century. The business grew so quickly that by 1852 the Soho Square premises had become too small, and Routledge moved to Farringdon Street.

'No. 36 was very quiet after Routledge had gone. The next known inhabitant of this house too was a bookseller, but a very different type. Mr John Russell Smith was known throughout the trade as "Antiquity Smith"; he was a recognised authority on English topography, genealogy and anonymous literature.'[23] So wrote Margaret Goldsmith in her history of Soho Square, published in 1947. In the 1930s the building was occupied by

'A Cosmopolitan News-stall off Leicester Square', in Paul Cohen-Portheim, *The Spirit of London*, 1935.

the Music Department of Oxford University Press, which moved to the square in 1935.

While the square increasingly became home to film companies such as Twentieth Century Fox and British Movietone News, publishing nonetheless continued to play an important role in Soho, due to its newsagents being famed for the variety of their offerings. Despite paper shortages and rationing, the newsagent was a main feature of Soho, as described by Stanley Jackson in 1946: 'Into Morioni's and similar newsagents go men and women of half a dozen nationalities. They buy an astonishing variety of newspapers and magazines, anything from the *Matrimonial Times* to *Nuite et Jour* . . . Fierce looking cyclists, undressed blondes, boxers with bulging muscles, and the newest surrealist painter stare at you from a dozen slim periodicals'.[24]

The influx of immigrants naturally added to the variety of trades existing in Soho. To cater for the French for example – the entrepreneurs, professionals, tailors, chefs and waiters, among other trades – there were French shops in Soho selling wooden shoes, berets and everything the connoisseur of French food and drink would want.

Specific groups of immigrants often took on particular trades, although the choice of trade was not always the most obvious. Jews, for example, were not particularly heavy drinkers, but there was an unusually high number of Jewish publicans in the area. The correlation between the two is not entirely clear, but perhaps it was the apparent profitability of public houses, and the poor working conditions of tailors, that led many West End Jews to become publicans. It was sometimes against their own instincts:

My grandfather was shocked at the idea. He had never been in a pub in his life, and any drinking he wanted was done with a few friends and a glass or two of schnapps. The idea of making a livelihood in a pub was abhorrent to him, and anyway he could hardly speak English. He was a little man, barely five feet tall, and a circumference to match. Hardly the idea of an English 'Mine Host'.

The offices of Robins, Gore & Mercer, auctioneers and surveyors, 205 Wardour Street. Photograph in G. C. Wilton, *The Story of Soho*, 1925.

However, his friend persuaded him . . . an interview was arranged, and before he knew it he was the licensee of the Hercules Pillars in Greek Street.[25]

Quite a few Soho residents made their living as a pub landlord. At the turn of the century the temperance reformer Arthur Sherwell counted seventy-six pubs in eighteen Soho streets. In 1894 the Metropolitan Police C Division, which covered the area of Soho and its immediate surroundings, contained 357 pubs and beer houses and 192 other premises with on- or off-licences. There were 545 licensed premises in an area of seven-tenths of a square mile. However, a drastic tightening of licensing laws in the early years of the twentieth century was to reduce the number of Soho's pubs to around fifty.

Many of Soho's more traditional industries were arguably in decline by the late nineteenth century. Reverend Cardwell's turn-of-the-century account of Soho history proudly proclaimed that many of the old trades such as Hopkins & Purvis (the oil colourmen of Greek Street), or Burroughes & Watts (the billiard makers of Soho Square), were still present. However, Wardour Street, he noted, traditionally a hub of furniture making and formerly home to the showrooms of Thomas Sheraton, had now taken on a more sinister character – Soho artisans were tending to focus their energies on producing fake antiquities for the increasing number of customers who had developed an interest in things such as Georgian fittings, signified by 'Chippendale', 'Sheraton' and 'Adam'.[26]

Some aspects of Soho's fin-de-siècle industrial production could therefore be described as a story of fraudulent activity and decaying commerce. Nonetheless, Soho was still home to booksellers and printers, leather sellers and saddlers, the famous jam manufacturers Crosse & Blackwell of Soho Square, and the world-renowned music publisher Novello of Wardour Street.

While some traditional industries left the area, new ones arrived. Although the large British film studios had been located

Wardour Street in the 1920s. Photograph by Lasky Film Service Ltd., published in G. C. Wilton, *The Story of Soho*, 1925.

since the 1920s in places that were further afield, such as Ealing, Soho's Wardour Street became the centre of British film production offices, post-production facilities and distribution companies. Soho residents frequently witnessed the arrivals of film stars, but they also often suffered the repetitive noises made by the film editors. Michael Klinger remembered 'it was particularly bad in summer when everybody's windows were open . . . we'd lean out of the window and yell at them to shut up'.[27]

But in the 1950s there were still many traces of the traditional industries resident in Soho. Those watchmakers and jewellers who had not moved to Clerkenwell and Hatton Garden were often involved in costume jewellery. 'Windows were lined with trays of glass beads, Marcasite brooches and imitation pearls on offer at 39s a dozen.'[28] Jewish tailors still dominated the area around Berwick Street, where cutters, pressers and buttonholers worked in small, hot and crowded workshops above the tailors' shops.

The area also had many music shops, such as Barney's in Shaftesbury Avenue. Stanley Jackson, writing in 1946, vividly evokes the Soho music scene at the time. At Barneys, he writes, 'you can buy anything from a uke string to a set of Chinese blocks for your drum'. It was just after the Second World War, and Barney's was one of the places attracting 'young jivers', who made 'a bee-line for the sax shop' to 'talk swing and run caressing fingers over the shiny instruments'. Many of these youngsters wore 'violent cravats, tied in a big, floppy knot, very light belted jackets, dark flannel trousers and suede shoes. They look under-nourished and their hair strays wildly over eyes that seem glazed by this strange musical pipe-dream.'[29]

Nonetheless, by the middle of the twentieth century there were concerns that the character of Soho had been lost. Some commentators lamented that Soho, 'like almost all other parts of London has lost all signs of leisure and easiness . . . Soho today is essentially a place of business'.[30] Whereas this may have been true for some parts of the district during the day, the story was a very different one at night.

Soho by Night

Not all Sohoites made a living by legal means, and the area achieved notoriety above all for its criminal underworld and nightlife. A commentary from the 1950s observed: 'It is difficult to say exactly when the neighbourhood first became the haunt of vice it is today. But by the twentieth century the names of its citizens were more likely to fill the calendar at the Old Bailey than the pages of Debrett.'[31] Fifty years earlier there were fears that respectable tenants were being turned out of their homes in favour of those involved in vice who would pay higher rents.[32] In 1907 G. R. Sims wrote, in his *Watches of the Night*, that Soho was:

> a refuge for the terrorists of the continent who have fled to avoid their own police. It has two or three streets which are chiefly inhabited by criminals. In it are clubs frequented by men who are violent and lawless, and a constant source of anxiety and trouble . . . The gambling dens of Soho are among the most difficult with which the authorities have to deal, many of them being carried on at the back of quite respectable looking shops . . . and these dens are frequented by some of the most disorderly and disreputable aliens who abuse our hospitality.[33]

As Jerry White points out, London's underworld 'was, in reality, many little underworlds which overlapped in Soho', and London's migrant communities either brought their own terrorists with them or 'grew them *in situ*'.[34] Soho was increasingly becoming not only the prime location for protection rackets, but also a leisure centre for the underworld. British Italian criminal Charles 'Darby' Sabini (notorious for his racecourse protection rackets)

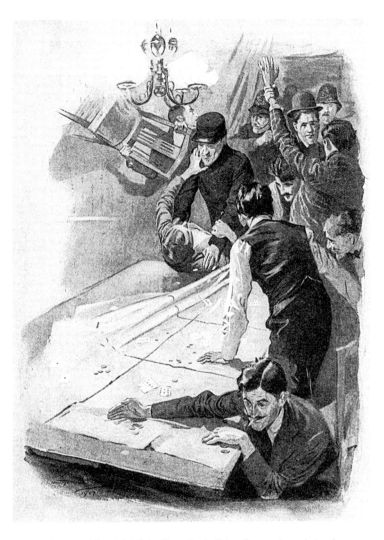

Police raiding a gambling club in Soho. Illustration by Sidney Seymour Lucas in *London Magazine*, October 1907.

and his four sons from Clerkenwell made Soho their territory in the 1920s. Both the Sabinis and their rivals the Cortesi brothers extorted protection from Little Italy's drinking clubs, whereas the 'Triads' took a share of Chinatown's gambling clubs. With its range of businesses and workers potentially crossing the divide between the lawful and the unlawful – such as bookmakers, nightclub proprietors, prostitutes and landlords of dubious reputation – Soho was the ideal location from which to operate such racketeering.

Throughout the twentieth century Soho's reputation persisted. A 1946 guidebook explained that a certain amount of organised crime was 'only to be expected in a slum district teeming with good hide-outs, where it is still possible to live cheaply and where men can meet and whisper "business" in quiet café bars and clubs without being noticed'. Crime flourished in 'the little café in Dean Street or the booze-parlours which a policeman cannot penetrate without a membership card or a couple of axes'.[35]

The true extent of criminal activities in the area was, however, difficult to gauge. Despite Soho's night-time reputation, there were many people living in the area, representing a range of nationalities, who were simply trying to scrape together an honest living. The writer and broadcaster Daniel Farson thought Soho's reputation for crime, vice and sex was at least in parts an invention of the press: '"The square mile of vice" was an easy label, used by two Sunday columnists in particular who delighted in giving Soho a bad name by presenting a scene of exaggerated violence with drug addicts, gambling dens, razor slashing, wide boys, and unspeakable sex.' When considering attempts by Sohoites to make a living by committing crime, 'Soho's reputation was worse than the reality'.[36] Stanley Jackson, writing in 1946, agreed: 'A murder in Soho automatically grabs the headline: but if someone is killed in Surbiton the victim must be content with a paltry ration of newsprint. It is just another murder.'[37]

However, some of the most notorious crimes committed in London did take place in Soho. The ever-present danger to prostitutes, and the likelihood of their experiencing violence at the hands of men who hated women, was highlighted in the 1930s when there had been a series of unsolved murders – in 1935 a French woman, 'Fifi', was strangled in a Soho flat, a year later Jeanette Cotton was strangled with a silk scarf and Constance Hind was battered with a flat iron, a thin wire around her neck, and in 1937 another French woman, 'Marie', was strangled in a blazing flat.[38]

No perpetrator was ever found in the case of these Soho women. Savage attacks on women of the trade in Soho also took place during the Second World War. In one week in February 1942 Gordon Frederick Cummins killed three prostitutes in their rooms in Soho, Fitzrovia and Paddington (although the exact number of women he killed remains unknown). All were brutally assaulted, strangled and grotesquely mutilated, thereby vividly resurrecting the memory of Jack the Ripper. Cummins was hanged in June 1942 at Wandsworth Prison. Just over twenty years later there was another case of serial murders of West End prostitutes. Six women were murdered between January 1964 and January 1965. Some of the victims were discovered naked on the Thames foreshore, which prompted the press to refer to their unknown assailant as 'Jack the Stripper'.

The disruption and dislocation of life during the London Blitz, and during the Second World War overall, arguably gave rise to two phenomena in London generally and Soho in particular – violent crime, and young criminals. Protection rackets and armed robberies especially received boosts from the war, and Soho was the most contentious area of London. The five Messina brothers from Malta ran a prostitution ring from the 1930s to the 1950s. During the war and immediately thereafter the five White brothers filled the Sabinis' shoes, extorting ransoms from clubs and gambling dens. Their reign was replaced by that of two rival gang leaders, Billy Hill and Jack Comer, until Comer was forced out – violently – leaving Billy Hill in an unchallenged position.

Career criminals and journalists at a party at Gennaro's restaurant in Soho, given by Billy Hill to launch his autobiography, *Boss of Britain's Underworld*, in 1955. Left to right: Soho Ted, Bugsy, Groin Frankie, Billy Hill, Ruby Sparkes, Frankie Fraser, College Harry, Frany the Spaniel, Cherry Bill, Johnny Ricco, a female journalist, Russian Ted and a publisher. A journalist is at the piano. Photograph by Bert Hardy, published in *Picture Post*, 3 December 1955.

Hill is described as combining 'the bloodthirsty capacity for terror so valuable to the protection racketeer . . . with a schoolman's skill at organisation and planning'.[39] He was behind a number of high-profile robbery cases, including the 1952 ambush of a post-office van in Marylebone, which earned Hill's men an unprecedented £287,000 in cash. The Betting and Gaming Act of 1960, designed to control London's gambling, transformed illegal gatherings in Soho back rooms into multi-million pound industries, opening the doors to protection rackets run by notorious gangs such as the Krays.

By the middle of the twentieth century the stereotype of the Soho criminal was firmly established, and 'spivs' were a common sight: 'They are the men who have no fixed occupation and live on their wits. They divide humanity into two classes, "wide" (smart in the criminal sense) and "steamers" (mugs). Your spiv is always a snappy dresser.'[40] According to a 1947 article in *Tailor & Cutter*, the spiv, found in great numbers in Soho, was 'a vulgarian and to him music only means jazz, colour means scarlets and yellows, talking means cursing, eating means gorging, drinking means soaking and dressing means fantastic exhibitionism'.[41]

This newly emerging trend, although linked by the press to crime, was in fact mostly created by law-abiding youths who congregated in Soho. It was the tailors of Soho who supplied this youth trend, often with cheap clothing. This partly explains why the area became the centre of Britain's post-war youth culture.

Aside from the types of crime described above, Soho's unsavoury reputation was caused by the sex trade, which had become firmly established in the area by the mid-nineteenth century. The women engaged in this trade came from a broad range of backgrounds, reflecting the overall spectrum of London society. In the 1880s around half of London's prostitutes were born in London, and records indicate that it was often poverty and poor working conditions in other trades that lured women into prostitution. For many young girls prostitution offered a way out of the London slums, leading them to ignore the occupational hazards such as disease, violence and even murder. Despite the harsh punishments meted out for sodomy, male prostitutes also frequented Soho in large numbers – as became public during the Oscar Wilde trials, which revealed details of restaurants in Rupert Street and the Café Royal where Wilde met boys brought to him by friends and pimps.

Some of London's most notorious centres of sexual commerce – 'night houses', brothels and assembly rooms such as the Argyll Rooms at Great Windmill Street – were located in Soho. By the 1860s the Argyll was the most famous dance saloon in the capital. On the gallery above the dance floor army officers, gentlemen and aristocrats fraternised with high-class courtesans. William Ewart Gladstone, then Chancellor of the Exchequer, was so concerned about the Argyll Rooms that he waited outside at night in one of his early efforts to save fallen women – 'save one for me, the old music-hall joke would go'.[42] He regularly took prostitutes back to his home, ensuring they had a meal and a bed for the night. One night in 1853 Gladstone met a prostitute in Long Acre and accompanied her back to her lodgings in (what was then) King Street. 'Opinion is divided as to whether he saved prostitutes or merely saved them until later'.[43] Whatever his intentions were, once they reached the house a young man approached Gladstone threatening to make public that he had picked up a prostitute unless he either gave him money or secured him a job. Gladstone, having nothing to hide, took the man to court where he was sentenced to twelve months hard labour.

Due to its shady reputation, the Argyll Rooms lost its battle to maintain its licence in 1878, but this certainly did not mean the end of prostitution in the area. The demise of London's other outdoor prostitution hotspots (such as Cremorne Gardens in Chelsea and the Vauxhall Pleasure Gardens), along with the rise of the West End music halls (which had been firmly associated with prostitution from the beginning), led to an increase of the number of prostitutes working in Soho. By the 1890s the promenades of the Alhambra Theatre and the Empire Theatre were, as Jerry White describes them, 'the premier showcase of well-dressed prostitution in London'.[44]

Street prostitution in the West End was also endemic, but whereas the working-class prostitutes were easily recognised by their obvious soliciting, higher class courtesans frequenting Regent Street were often hard to distinguish from respectable women, as expressed by one customer's account of the 1860s:

> One summer's morning about midday, I was in the Quadrant . . . In front of me I saw a well-grown woman . . . She was holding her petti-coats well up out of the dirt, the common habit of even respectable women then. With gay ladies the habit was to hold them up just a little higher. . . she stopped, and looked into a shop. 'Is she gay?' I thought. 'No.' . . . She looked at me but the look was so steady, indifferent, and with so little of the gay woman in her expression, that I could not make up my mind as to whether she was accessible or not . . . I followed quickly, saying as I came close, 'Will you come with me?' She made no reply, and I fell behind. Soon she stopped again at a shop . . . and again I said, 'May I go with you?' 'Yes – where to?'[45]

This behaviour could make it very difficult for respectable women to frequent the area, as they were often approached by men looking for sex.

The Great War put an end to some aspects of Soho's nightlife by introducing watered down alcohol and stricter licensing laws. But the impact of both world wars on the sex trade in Soho was clear. In a city that became both an international intersection and renowned centre of entertainment for troops passing through, a climate of greater promiscuity created a high demand for prostitution. Soho in particular replaced the main promenades of the West End as a place for prostitutes to congregate. It was in the inter-war period that 'the peculiar closed-in world of ponce and prostitute became one of the defining features of twentieth-century Soho'.[46]

By the end of the Second World War there were so many prostitutes that a former Soho resident of the time recalled that, 'as a kid coming home from school, I had to say "Excuse me" to get to my own front door'.[47] Francis Bacon recalled that 'the prostitutes were all over the streets. The streets were more fun, more amusing. The prostitutes gave a living sense to the streets.'[48] This, however, changed dramatically with the 1959 Street Offences Act, which made soliciting illegal and literally emptied the streets overnight.

But of course the trade continued, and the busker Henry Hollis recalled:

> Soho in the middle of the night long after the spivs and prostitutes have gone to bed . . . Young girls who have left home for the bright lights, just walking around with an old battered suitcase. Maybe just around the corner there are ponces waiting for a likely girl to put on the game. It is their best time in the middle of the night to catch a young girl straight awf [sic] of the train from up norf [sic]. They would promise her all sorts and next thing she knew she was on the game working for some ponce who never had the decency to earn an honest living.[49]

The 1959 Act, designed to clear prostitutes off the streets, essentially forced them into the arms of pimps and organised criminals, who now set up 'hostess bars' where clients could meet prostitutes. The profits made in the process from entrance fees and exorbitant prices for mock-champagne, non-alcoholic wine and 'near beer' effectively meant the government had provided the Soho underworld with a licence to print money. At the same time, the 1959 Obscene Publications Act meant that finally the pornography business, hitherto discreetly tucked away in back rooms, came out in the open.

A group of people peer into the window of a club offering 'non-stop striptease' in Walkers Court, 1965. Photograph by Chris Ware.

Public concerns that innocent young girls could meet a terrible fate in London were also closely linked to Soho. 'White slavery', one of the biggest fears of so-called 'respectable London', dated back to at least the early twentieth century. Many London parents feared their daughters would be lured into Soho, where they would be drugged and put on a cargo ship to work as prostitutes in South America, or else taken to a house in a London neighbourhood unknown to them, where they would be ill-treated by villainous men and then thrown out in the middle of the night as 'ruined' women. A former superintendent of the CID, however, remained unconvinced that this was a widespread phenomenon, and thought that 'some girls rely on a somewhat vivid but limited imagination in order to excuse their voluntary absence from home when confronted by anxious and loving parents'.[50]

The Jewish Association for the Protection of Girls and Women claimed that in 1900 there had been 125 cases of young Jewish women being shipped to Cairo and Buenos Aires having fled the pogroms of Eastern Europe and come to London, and that by 1902 the number had doubled. It was accepted, however, that many of the women had already been prostitutes before coming to England, and that in most cases they had not been shipped against their will. Vigilance committees and journalists nonetheless helped stoke the fears. The journalist George Sims claimed that Soho contained 'a well-organised syndicate that loitered in milliners' and dress shops specifically to recruit English girls'.[51] Naturally this kind of reporting increased the hostility against foreigners that was already evident at the time.

Concerns over white slavery led to the establishment of a White Slave Traffic Squad in 1912, which reported a year later that 'there has been an utter absence of evidence to justify these alarming statements'.[52] There had apparently been no cases of innocent girls being kidnapped; the girls were Jewish women of Russian or Polish origin, who went to Argentina and Brazil.

Soho's association with drug-related crime was also notorious throughout the nineteenth and twentieth centuries. Cocaine, introduced to London in bulk by Canadian soldiers during the First World War, became a serious concern on the home front, as it was feared it would undermine morale. The *Evening News* reported, in 1916, that 'Cocaine has dangers for women apart from its ruinous effect on the nervous system. It is fatal to self-discipline and therefore a predisposing cause of moral as well as physical destruction'.[53]

Once trade with cocaine became illegal, Soho became a key centre for the supply of the drug. Twenty-six-year-old one-legged Willie Johnson, who lived with a prostitute in New Compton Street, found himself on the receiving end of the first ever recorded London drug bust, when he dropped eleven boxes of cocaine while trying to escape police officers. In 1923 S. T. Felstead, in his *The Underworld of London*, declared that, prior to the First World War, 'the thought of a West End night club haunted by negroes and China-men peddling poisonous drugs to stupid women would have aroused a thrill of horror', whereas 'today it happens that some pleasure sated girl dies from an overdose of cocaine or morphine, supplied to her by some black or yellow parasite, and people merely shrug their shoulders'.[54]

One of the first and most well-known Chinese drug dealers supplying Soho and the West End was Chan Nan, or 'Brilliant Chang', described as 'a stocky figure scarcely five feet tall with patent-leather shoes and a fur-collared melton cloth coat', who operated a drug-trafficking business from his restaurant premises on 107 Regent Street.[55] Highly educated, and speaking several languages, he came to London in 1913 to help look after his uncle's business interests, which included the Regent Street restaurant.

Becoming extremely successful in trafficking both drugs and women, Chang was thought to be the supplier of the cocaine which led to at least two high-profile deaths in London. Billie Carlton, a beautiful young actress described by the *Sunday Pictorial* as 'a frail beauty and delicate . . . all of that perishable, moth like substance that does not last long in the wear and tear of this rough and ready world', collapsed and died after the Victory Ball at the Albert Hall just after the end of the First World War.[56] In March 1922 Brilliant Chang appeared in court over the death of Freda Kempton, a young dancing instructor who also died of an overdose of cocaine. There was not enough evidence to link him to the death and, according to the *News of the World*, when the jury acquitted him, 'Chang smiled broadly and quickly left the court. As he passed out several well-dressed girls patted his shoulder while one ran her fingers through his hair'.[57]

After a succession of police raids Chang sold the restaurant and became a partner in the Palm Court Club in Gerrard Street, before moving on to a dilapidated property in the East End. He was finally arrested in 1924, after one of his couriers who brought the drugs from his premises in Limehouse to Soho by taxi was caught and revealed his name under pressure. Chan was finally deported to China in April 1925.

Of course not all of Soho's nightlife was associated with crime. Soho's reputation for its international cuisine – or, in the words of Thomas Burke, 'London's escape from English cooking'[58] – in turn constituted the backbone of the area's reputation as London's prime entertainment hotspot. Much of Soho's culinary trade was fuelled by the hard work of generations of immigrants, most of whom were from Italy and France. As the travel writer Mrs Eliza Cook wrote in 1902, every year many Italian migrants underwent a 'cruel and comfortless expatriation' from 'their romantic valleys to our foggy shores', where the 'worn and shabby' arrivals queued in a 'pitiful black line of seedy applicants' for work in one of the West End's many restaurants such as Monico, Gatti's or Oddenino's.[59]

The social investigator Charles Booth found the wide range of wages paid in the catering industry towards the end of the nineteenth century quite remarkable. Depending on skills, training, experience and the status of the employer, his survey recorded earnings from £2 to £20 per week for cooks and cellarmen ('it goes without saying that the majority of chefs are French'), £1 to £20 for waiters and 6s to 12s for kitchen and scullery boys.[60] Press revelations in the first decade of the twentieth century about unhygienic conditions and exploitative labour practices did not advance Soho's reputation. Stories of adulterated food prepared in rat-infested underground kitchens and served by 'deracinated foreigners' were increasingly seen as emblematic of the 'devious, vicious, dirtily-pleasant, exoticism' of the district.[61]

Soho also increasingly featured in debates about the displacement of British workers by foreign waiters. Prior to the Great War, the press increasingly accused German waiters of being spies. One outcome of this xenophobic resentment was the formation of the Loyal British Waiters Society in 1910, whose aim was clearly to remove foreigners from the trade. But the working conditions in the industry – which Charles Booth thought 'offensive to manly traditions of the English' – ensured that there was a steady supply of foreign waiters in Soho.[62] This supply would only be curtailed by the advent of two world wars.

Transformations

Soho's economy was made up of a curious and highly diverse array of trades, turning the area into a busy hub that sustained ordinary workers and traders but also prostitutes and criminals both during the day and at night. Many of Soho's traditional industries such as the furniture trade were nearly as old as the area itself, and some managed to survive into the twentieth century. Others disappeared and were replaced with those businesses brought on by the rapidly developing technologies of the twentieth century, such as the film industry.

But of course there was much more to Soho than its retail businesses and industries. Towards the end of the nineteenth century the area was transformed into London's premier hub for entertainment – restaurants, theatres, cinemas and of course Soho's infamous nightlife. Increasingly, instead of being a district where ordinary people made a living, Soho became a magnet for visitors from all over London, Britain and the world who were looking for entertainment of all kinds. It is this exciting world of entertainment, that so often broke with social norms and conventions, which gave Soho its notoriety and allure. It is now time to step into the history of this world and discover why Soho is famous throughout the world.

'Audience Cheering the Election Results at the Alhambra.' Drawing by H. M. Paget in the *Sphere*, 10 December 1910. The original caption describes how audiences gathered in theatres to hear the general election results of December 1910. At the Empire Theatre 'men in evening dress ran down the aisles of the stalls to inform their friends of the results, waving papers as they ran'. *The Times* is quoted as saying: 'At the Alhambra, when the first gain was shown to be Liberal something like a groan went up from a full house'. The Liberals won the election by a slim majority.

Chapter 4 **World of Arts and Entertainment**

Although many of Soho's streets in the nineteenth century were mired in poverty, the area increasingly became famous as an entertainment district with unique offerings for very little expense. Writing in 1911 and looking back over the previous twenty years, one writer felt that London's pleasure seekers cherished Soho 'as a place for wonderful and inexpensive meals in foreign restaurants, and a convenient centre for the various places of amusement, be they Theatres or Music Halls'.[1]

By the 1950s, Soho had acquired fame as an iconic amusement hub. The antique dealer and scene-maker Christopher Gibbs remembered that, from the 1950s onwards, Chelsea Setters – 'famous for what they were seen wearing: ethnic outfits from colonial outposts, exaggerated versions of gentlemen's clothes from previous generations of English fashion; colourful, form-fitting trousers and flowing shirts, even blue jeans, then generally worn mainly by labourers' – migrated into Soho for entertainment, 'where you could feel some of the upsurging change'. After the Second World War, Gibbs recalled, 'Soho was, along with Chelsea, the one place in London where you could count on running into artists, writers, drunks, loons, and the daft on a regular basis – with the difference that in Soho you also rubbed shoulders with gangsters, pimps, hookers, strippers, pornographers and slumming actors from nearby West End theatres'. He described how the area's restaurants, bars, pubs, cafés and nightclubs had turned Soho into a place of 'hardcore bohemia', a place where:

> foreigners ran the restaurants and pubs, where homosexuals felt relatively safe, where vice businesses were permitted if not free rein, then certainly lots of elbow room . . . There were East End kids coming up for a good time in the West End. There were jazz clubs and night spots and coffee bars and a sprinkling of gay bars and such. It drew a lot of people from the provinces and east London.[2]

It is the story of Soho's places of entertainment that this chapter explores. The contrast between 'light and dark' added to the mystery and allure of Soho's entertainment and nightlife. From the early twentieth century onwards, Soho's darkness stood in stark contrast to the brightness of the main streets surrounding it. In 1910 Westminster Council employed the Gas Light and Coke Company to install lights of 1,800 and 3,000 candlepower along the streets that bordered Soho. By contrast, Soho's own lampposts were fitted with 90 candlepower lamps. Robert Machray, author of *The Night Side of London*, commented in 1902 that Soho held 'more of the night side of London than all the rest of it put together'.[3] For some Soho revellers, the 'idea of the darkness was that you'd be dancing with someone else's husband and your husband was across the room with the man's wife'.[4]

Arguably Soho's rise to fame is in large part due to its restaurants and theatres, so a few examples of the many establishments of the area form the starting point of this journey into the history of Soho's world of entertainment, followed by some of the pubs and bars so revered by London's bohemia as well as the rich and famous. Naturally the nightclubs, coffee bars and cafés, as well as the seedier, 'darker' nature of amusement in the form of strip clubs, are also part of this story.

Restaurants

Although the term 'restaurant' was hardly used in London guidebooks prior to 1875 – as eating out largely took place in inns, taverns and coffee houses – Soho was one of the first areas in London where this foreign import took hold. According to one journalist, Soho's restaurants in the 1870s were frequented by foreigners, artists, poets and 'other degenerate Englishmen'.[5]

Gerrard Street became the centre of Soho's culinary explosion, and it is most likely that it was the Mont Blanc Restaurant – the first place serving French cuisine – that attracted the English gourmand. By 1886 Baedecker's guidebook was advising its readers that 'there are many cheap and good foreign restaurants in Soho'.[6] Blanchard's Restaurant in Beak Street, formerly a famous coaching house, had a no-ladies-after-five policy. It became a nightclub in 1913. Charles Dickens attended a birthday party at the restaurant, in honour of Ellen Ternan, his mistress, shortly before his death.

Soho's most famous restaurants around the turn of the century were Kettner's in Romilly Street, French restaurants including Maxim's in Wardour Street, Coventry Street and Old Compton Street, and the Italian restaurants in Rupert Street, Gerrard Street and Old Compton Street. Kettner's was founded in 1867 by Auguste Kettner, who had previously worked as chef to the French emperor Napoleon III. Its fame spread after a positive review in *The Times* and the restaurant became something of a national institution, soon producing the iconic *Kettner's Book of the Table*, with recipes supplied by Kettner himself. Edward VII favoured the place for secret meetings with his mistress, the actress Lillie Langtry.

The relatively inexpensive Solferino's in Rupert Street was a favourite of the caricaturist and writer Max Beerbohm. Described as 'the greatest of English comic artists' by *The Times*, Beerbohm was the subject of one of the finest paintings by artist William

KETTNER'S

Restaurant Telephone: GERRARD 3437
Banquets   "   "   6437

ROMILLY STREET
SOHO - LONDON - W1

Bill for Kettner's Restaurant, 1920.

Nicholson, another frequent visitor to Solferino's. Also in Rupert Street was the Florence, a celebrity haunt of the early twentieth century, favoured decadent destination and a regular haunt of the Welsh writer Arthur Machen. His novel *The Hill of Dreams* is described by the *Oxford Dictionary of National Biography*, as 'one of the period's most lyrical and decadent novels'.[7] Oscar Wilde entertained one of his teenage lovers at the Florence, with champagne in a private dining room.

As early as the turn of the century, many of Soho's restaurants offered a 'darker side' of entertainment. Some establishments had *cabinets particulier*, where customers could enjoy a meal and sex in a private room. 'If you pay 10 shillings extra, you are not bothered there.'[8] Italian restaurants in particular were linked to Soho's sex trade in the inter-war period. The journalist Sidney Moseley commented in 1920 that many Picadilly *demin-mondaines* 'made their headquarters on the upper floor of "bohemian restaurants"'.[9]

Attempts to make Soho more gastronomically upmarket were unsuccessful, as demonstrated by the Pelican Club. Previously located in Denman Street, the Pelican Club moved into a purpose-built club house in Gerrard Street in 1889. The *Survey of London, Volumes 33 and 34*, published by London County Council in 1966, describes the building in some detail. The new club house was arranged 'on an entirely novel principle, consisting practically of three large and lofty rooms, connected by a grand 5ft staircase . . . built in the rooms themselves, and quite open'. In the basement was a gymnasium 'for boxing entertainments and other amusements', while the ground floor accommodated the general club-room and the first floor a billiard room. On the roof 'was a glass construction used as a smoking-lounge in summer'.[10]

Despite its grand design, the Pelican Club went bankrupt after only three years, and the building was sold. This was partly due to breaches of the licensing laws and partly due to complaints by local residents, as outlined in *The Times* in September 1890:

'noise occasioned by contests in the prize ring of the club and the crowds which such contests caused to assemble in the street, smoking concerts, whistling for cabs, and other alleged annoyances'.[11]

It was only in the brightly lit area of Leicester Square that grand dining was a success at this time, in such establishments as Scott's, the Trocadero and Lyons' Corner House. The rise of Soho's theatre industry provided a further impetus to the area's restaurant scene, as increasingly not only theatregoers but also the stars of the stage themselves regularly ventured into Soho after performances. Meanwhile the Mont Blanc in Gerrard Street had become a meeting place for a literary circle that included Joseph Conrad. Hilaire Belloc met G. K. Chesterton there for the first time in 1900.

Although Soho was traditionally dominated by French flavours, it was Italian cuisine that became increasingly popular in the twentieth century. Pepino Leoni's Quo Vadis restaurant in Dean Street developed a unique atmosphere in the inter-war period, when in 1929 the artist Edward Carrick proposed that he and his friends use it as an exhibition space as they had previously done in a restaurant in Paris. They formed an artist society – the 'Grubb Group' – which was limited to sixteen members and displayed art on the walls of Leoni's restaurant. Members were given meal vouchers by Leoni – 'for grub, if you like!', as Edward Carrick explained. The first exhibition consisted of over 100 paintings. The combination of Italian food and art was a huge success, with the *Daily Express* proclaiming that 'Soho has its own Academy'.[12]

The success of the concept of artists painting in order to eat allowed Leoni to expand Quo Vadis across three houses on Dean Street, including the one that had contained the two cramped rooms rented by Karl Marx before his move to Hampstead. The Grubb Group therefore played a key role in extending the link between art and restaurants that had been established as early as the 1890s, when artists used Soho's establishments as

Pepino Leoni seen here in his restaurant, Quo Vadis, on Dean Street. Unattributed photograph in the *Sketch*, 17 December 1958. A native of Cannero, on the shores of Lake Maggiore, Leoni arrived in London in 1907. He learned his trade as a kitchen boy and then waiter, before opening his restaurant in 1926.

their social headquarters. Quo Vadis continued this tradition in the 1930s when it became a regular haunt of writers such as H. G. Wells and Max Beerbohm, as well as film star Moira Shearer, West End actress Evelyn Laye and cabaret star Alice Delysia.

According to a contemporary issue of *Country Life*, 1930s Soho possessed a 'subtle atmosphere', which told visitors that:

> here you will find macaroni instead of rice, and veal more plentiful than beef. There is an oiliness about the place which speaks to your material senses of ragouts rather than of stews; of potatoes capable of being transformed into a hundred forms; of a cunning in the concoction of sauces; of ravioli and spaghetti; of perennial chickens; and the garnishing of watercress, and almost impossibly green lettuces.[13]

Not all of inter-war Soho's Italian restaurants were as subtle or as tasteful as Quo Vadis. At the Taverna Medicea all the staff wore Renaissance costumes, while Gennaro's was furnished with extravagant lamp-shades that were shaped and coloured like birds. What restaurants like Quo Vadis provided was 'some of the best Italian cooking in London', which, according to *London Week*, offered refined dishes that 'originated in Italy, but are adapted to the universal taste by the elimination of strong flavours'.[14] However, an Italian waiter who worked at Quo Vadis in the 1950s was rather less complimentary towards the food, saying that 'it was not Italian ... [Leoni] used to take French dishes and put an Italian name, like *Pollo alla Principessa* instead of *Poulet a la Princesse*. That was not Italian food at all to me'.[15]

The outbreak of war in 1939 brought about changes to Soho's restaurant trade, but did not spell the end of it. Jack Isow's small café in Walker's Court had opened in 1938, but after American GIs began to arrive in Soho he expanded his business, eventually taking over the entirety of Walker's Court. Increasingly attracting celebrities, it became London's premier Jewish restaurant, and the only one to attract non-Jewish customers. One contemporary

A disappointed Jack Solomons, boxing promoter, sitting between two empty places reserved for boxers Billy Stephens and Ralph Dupas who had failed to turn up for lunch at Isow's restaurant. Photographer unknown, 1962.

Evan. 6443

Curry, Curry, Curry.

R. BANKS,

2 & 3, Green Street, Leicester Square,

SERVES A REAL INDIAN CURRY

Daily from 12 to 3.

Tennyson wrote of the "Cock," and
Their plump head waiter,
Where often he used to resort
At the hour of five by his indicator
To indulge in a pint of old port.

I write of the Crown
Where men of renown,
To Banks' like good citizens hurry,
To lodge there their cash,
And receive not a hash,
But a luncheon of Real Indian Curry.

Friday, the Gt. Madras authority on Curry advises,
**Theom Curry Khana Koo Mungtha Banks Sab Ka
pass goue.**

Wines, Spirits and Malt Liquors of the highest character.

nov 5 1886

W. STRAKER, Printer, Ludgate Hill, E.C.

Advertisement for R. Banks restaurant, at 2–3 Green Street, Leicester Square, serving 'a real Indian curry', 1886.

remembered that 'all the celebrities came into Isow's Restaurant. All the boxing fraternity – Jack Solomons and the others. All the film actors and actresses – Danny Kaye, Betty Hutton, Frank Sinatra, and Walt Disney'.[16]

Although many Italian restaurateurs were arrested and interned when Italy declared war on Britain in 1940, Soho's Italian restaurants survived the war, often continuing as British-owned businesses. Many began to flourish again after 1945: 'The appetite for espresso and Italian fashions for men opened English eyes to a great many things', remembered restaurateur Alvaro Maccioni: 'They realised that on the other side of the channel there was life after the war . . . They didn't want to eat roast lamb any more . . . Before, food was like gas or electricity: then it became another form of entertainment.'[17] One commentator wrote in 1946 that, 'despite all the difficulties, the Soho restaurants are enjoying the biggest boom in their history'.[18]

In the 1950s Soho continued to be the best neighbourhood to haunt in search of ethnic food other than haute cuisine. According to one contemporary, diners in 1950s London were 'desperate for subtle variations on the austerity theme', and a 1956 guide listed over three dozen restaurants in Soho, eight of which were Italian, five French, four Chinese, three 'French and Italian', three Hungarian, two Indian and two Spanish.[19]

Soho's Theatres and Cinemas

The success of Soho's restaurants was increasingly linked to the thriving theatre business in the area. London's theatre industry established a firm foothold in Soho after the creation of Cambridge Circus, Charing Cross Road and Shaftesbury Avenue in the 1880s. The newly emerging theatres such as the Palace Theatre on Cambridge Circus and the Shaftesbury and Queen's Theatres on Shaftesbury Avenue placed Soho firmly at the centre of Theatreland. The theatre construction boom of the 1880s created London's answer to Broadway. The Prince of Wales was built in 1884, and the Garrick, Daly's, the Lyric and the Duke of York followed shortly thereafter. In 1886 the Criterion Theatre, the brainchild of actor-manager Charles Wyndham, also opened its doors. Still more theatres opened along Shaftesbury Avenue, with the Apollo, Globe and the Prince's attracting an increasingly middle-class clientele to Soho.

The Palace Theatre was built by theatre impresario Richard D'Oyly Carte at the immense cost of £150,000. The interior decorations boasted Mexican onyx and Italian marble, and there was even a 'royal retiring room'. Carte had previously enjoyed tremendous success by promoting Gilbert and Sullivan's work. The Royal English Opera House, as the theatre was originally known, opened with Sullivan's grand opera *Ivanhoe* on 31 January 1891. Unfortunately the production was a failure, and Carte had to sell the venue shortly thereafter. Sarah Bernhardt briefly featured at the theatre before it was transformed into one of London's most renowned variety theatres, with performances from Russian ballerina Anna Pavlova, comedians Wilkie Bard and Harry Champion, as well as juggler Paul Cinquevalli. Cinquevalli stunned his audiences by performing a 'human billard table' stunt in which he caught four balls and a wineglass in the pockets of his specially tailored jacket.

From the mid-nineteenth century onwards, Soho's history was therefore increasingly intertwined with the world of theatre. The London Palladium in Argyll Street began its life as an amusement arcade. It then became the Corinthian Bazaar and Exhibition Rooms in the 1860s, before being converted into Hengler's Circus. As a circus venue and ice-skating ring it provided a permanent home for Charles Hengler's touring circus. It was only in 1910 that it opened as a luxurious music hall designed by Frank Matcham, offering variety theatre. It cost £250,000 to build and offered features such as box-to-box telephones and a palm court in Norwegian granite behind the stalls. It soon turned into a revue theatre, hosting the Crazy Gang in the 1930s (described as a 'comic troupe of stage-hardened middle-aged males').[20] *Peter Pan* was first performed there at Christmas 1930, and was repeated every year until 1938. The Palladium achieved national fame from 1955 onwards with the television variety show, *Sunday Night at the London Palladium*.

Towards the end of the nineteenth century Leicester Square became home to the greatest cosmopolitan clubs in the world – the Alhambra Theatre and the Empire Theatre. It was in these two spaces that 'French visitors made their home in London, and where Englishmen could sometimes forget that they were English, yet never that they ruled the empire'. The poet Arthur Symons felt that the area was a 'sordid yet irresistible reminder of Paris and Italy'.[21]

As one of London's most famous theatres of the late Victorian period, the Alhambra went through many transformations throughout its existence and was known under eight different names in total. Opened in 1854 as The Royal Panopticon of Science and Art – 'an Institution for Scientific Exhibitions and for promoting discoveries in Arts and Manufactures' – it was the brainchild of the Irish scientific instrument-maker Edward Marmaduke Clarke, founder of the London Electrical Society. The building was designed to be a smaller version of the Great Exhibition of 1854, and cost the huge sum of £80,000 to build. Built in a 'Saracenic' or Moorish style, the striking exterior featured two minaret-like towers and a huge dome. The Panopticon contained a vast hall, a hydraulic lift and a thirty-metre high fountain supplied by a well underneath the building. The largest organ in England, built by Hill and Co., was installed, as well as copies of famous sculptures and mosaics.

Immediately after its opening over a thousand visitors a day paid a shilling to witness the scientific wonders on display, but unfortunately this did not last. The cholera epidemic raging in London at the time, as well as an incompetent management, contributed to the closure of the Panopticon after only two

Poster for Babil the Giant Amazon Queen and her companion Bijou at the Alhambra Theatre, Leicester Square. c.1900. Note the height chart on the right-hand side.

years. All the exhibits were sold off, including the organ (which went to St Paul's Cathedral). The building reopened in 1857 as the Alhambra Palace, a circus – Queen Victoria visited to see 'Black Eagle, the Horse of Beauty'. In 1860 the Alhambra became a music hall, and four years later Frederick Strange became manager, introducing the spectacular ballets which made the Alhambra famous.

Under Frederick Strange the theatre hosted the first ever performance in London of the French can-can – which promptly cost the Alhambra its dancing licence: 'Wiry Sal' had raised her foot 'higher than her head several times towards the audience and had been much applauded'.[22] The theatre was subsequently closed, but Strange was able to reopen it and use the venue for stage plays, comic opera and concerts instead.

A fire destroyed the Alhambra in 1882, but its reconstruction largely preserved the outer façade while dramatically increasing the capacity to 4,000 visitors, of whom 1,800 could be seated. Ballet and music hall were now the mainstay of the theatre, and the greatest successes included *The Bing Boys are Here* (1916) with George Robey, and the 1919 Diaghilev ballet season. In 1931 *Waltzes from Vienna* enjoyed a run of 607 performances, but it became increasingly evident that, like many of its rivals, the Alhambra was unable to compete with a new challenge – the advent of the cinema.

In 1936 the building was demolished to make way for the Odeon cinema, which was to be an equally impressive edifice. Its austere façade, made from black granite, was designed by Andrew Mather and Harry Weedon; the flanking tower is 120 feet high. The largest in the country, the cinema opened in 1937 with the film *The Prisoner of Zenda*, starring Ronald Colman. From 1939 to 1943 *Gone with the Wind* was played, making it the longest-running film of the Second World War. The Odeon was also the first cinema in Britain to install a wide screen, in 1953.

The Empire, the Alhambra's neighbour, opened its doors in 1884 after a brief stint as the Royal London Panorama, and its

Poster for *The Palace of Pearl* at the Empire Theatre, 1886.

career was similar to that of the Alhambra. Its exterior featured classic Renaissance architecture, but the interior featured lavish oriental designs. Initially starting as an opera house with high cultural ambitions, it was transformed into a theatre and then into a variety theatre, specialising in spectacular ballet performances with elaborate stage and costume design. The themes of the performances were often celebrations of Empire and the British military.

Audiences at the Empire were mostly seated but, as described in an account written in 1870, there was one area where men of a 'good class' entertained women who had entered the premises 'without the escort of a man' and slowly moved around the promenade to attract attention.[23] Erotic performances were part of the attraction of Soho theatres such as the Empire. *Tableaux vivants* – scenes enacted by nude female performers who would strike a pose and then stand motionless – provided erotic entertainment to men as early as the 1890s.

The reputation of the Empire became so notorious that it was targeted by a 'Purity Campaign', led by a Mrs Ormiston Chant in 1894. An attempt was made to separate the infamous promenade from the audience with screens to deter prostitutes, but an angry audience, led by none other than a youthful Winston Churchill, tore them down. Churchill wrote to his brother: 'Did you see the papers about the riot at the Empire last Saturday? It was I who led the rioters – and made a speech to the crowd – "Ladies of the Empire, I stand for Liberty!"'[24] The victory was short-lived, however, as one condition for renewing the Empire's licence was the alteration of the promenade to prevent soliciting.

After a successful career showing musical comedies in the years following the First World War, the Empire was transformed into the Empire Cinema in 1928. When it opened it boasted the largest auditorium in the West End. In 1929 over 82,000 customers visited the cinema in a single week, the highest number of any West End cinema ever.

'The Empire Promenade.' Illustration by Tom Browne, in Robert Machray, *The Night Side of London*, London 1920.

The Empire was by no means the only Soho theatre offering attractions to men looking for entertainment involving nude flesh. The first and most famous of Soho's establishments to display nudity on stage was the Windmill Theatre, opened in 1932 by Laura Henderson and her manager Vivian Van Damm. As the theatre struggled to survive with its initial 'rolling revue' programme of a 'non-stop show of flesh and blood vaudeville', Van Damm decided to follow the French: 'Nudes are the way forward'. It was the Windmill Theatre that broke down Victorian conventions where public nudity was regarded with outright horror. The Lord Chamberlain agreed that nudes could appear on the Windmill's stage – provided they remained static, and the presentations were 'wholly artistic'. The Windmill Theatre's attendances soared, and it would remain successful for three decades.[25]

Cafés

Soho became synonymous with yet another institution arriving in London in the twentieth century – the café. The traditional London coffee house had been superseded by the café by the early 1900s. Small round tables and chairs replaced the benches and square tables of the Victorian era. Soho's cafés began to thrive during the 1920s, offering meeting places for the area's 'thieves, fences, prostitutes, dope dealers and impecunious intellectuals'.[26]

The typical Soho café featured a mahogany-coloured horseshoe-shaped or lemon-shaped bar. They often stayed open late, as they were not affected by licensing laws, and therefore attracted increasing numbers of theatre- and cinema-goers throughout the inter-war period.

Soho's cafés were in their prime in the 1950s. According to a 1958 account, 'they bring a different character to Soho, they are the teenagers and skiffle merchants'.[27] London's very first coffee bar opened in Frith Street in 1953, and from the beginning the

Customers and staff at the Moka Bar, Frith Street, 21 August 1954. Photograph by Kurt Hutton, published in 'A Red-Head in Search of Black Coffee', *Picture Post*, 21 August 1954. The Moka was London's first espresso bar.

combination of Italian coffee, music from jukeboxes and artistic decorations proved popular with London's post-war generation. Heaven and Hell, which opened in 1956 in Old Compton Street, featured interior designs reflecting its name, while the Partisan in Carlisle Street provided a more intellectual ambience with chess boards and foreign newspapers.

London's most famous café, the 2i's Coffee Bar, was in Old Compton Street, and like many of Soho's cafés it increasingly provided live music. It was in the 2i's tiny windowless basement cellar that young working-class Britons were for the first time provided with a stage, and many skiffle and rock'n'roll talents were discovered. Bruce Welch, who arrived in London in 1958 and regularly played at the 2i's, recalled that 'Soho had become a Mecca for hundreds of young musicians who drifted into London from Manchester, Liverpool, Birmingham, Glasgow, and Newcastle, their only possession a guitar, all hoping to get work in the many coffee bars'.[28]

Cliff Richard, Tommy Steele and Billy Fury all first played to audiences in the basements of Soho's cafés.

Pubs and Soho-itis

A much older form of entertainment, which proved at least as popular as cafés, was provided by Soho's pubs. At the turn of the century the temperance reformer Arthur Sherwell counted seventy-six pubs in eighteen of Soho's streets – commenting of the streets 'most of which are exceedingly short'.[29] By the time of the First World War this number had fallen to around fifty, including the famous York Minster. Under German ownership until 1914, it was taken over by Victor Berlemont and quickly became known as 'the French pub'. It became a bohemian icon and for the next seventy-five years remained with the Berlemont family, who turned it into one of the most famous pubs in London.

Landlord Victor Berlemont with his pastis machine at the York Minster pub in Soho, October 1941. Photograph by Kurt Hutton, published in 'A Soho Pub is Unofficial Headquarters of Free French', *Picture Post*, 18 October 1941. The original caption explained: 'The device filters water through sugar and ice into glasses of neat pastis. The pub is popular with French citizens.'

Soho was also once home to the Crown Pub on Charing Cross Road. This was a favourite haunt of the decadents of the 'naughty nineties'. As it was so close to many of the West End theatres, such as the Empire and Alhambra, it became a convenient meeting place for 'a stimulating mixture of novelists, poets, painters, dramatists, showgirls, critics and hangers-on of the arts'. The Crown's customers 'drank hot gin and water' while talking 'learnedly about the ballet and Walter Sickert and the latest art movement in France'.[30] Among its regulars was Oscar Wilde, who drank hot port and had conversations with fellow exponents of the decadent movement such as Aubrey Beardsley and Ernest Dowson. The Crown later vanished in the redevelopment of Leicester Square tube station. Soho's pubs often attracted famous guests. George Orwell, for instance, drank at the Argyll Arms pub on Argyll Street, famed for its exuberant interior dating from 1895.

The Second World War led to an unexpected boost for some of Soho's pubs. After the fall of France in 1940, the York Minster became the unofficial London headquarters of the Free French, and many Allied soldiers who had visited the place as squaddies in the First World War now returned as officers – to find Victor Berlemont still behind the bar all those years later. The Dutch-run De Hems pub in Macclesfield Street provided a base for members of the Dutch resistance. As the French Pub was very small it often got very crowded, so many Sohoites favoured the much larger Helvetia in Old Compton Street. Despite the pub's rough reputation, the ex-detective inspector landlord never let things get out of hand. It was here in 1943 that the writer and journal editor Meary 'Tambi' Tambimuttu warned a friend to be beware of Soho: 'It is a dangerous place, you must be careful . . . You might get Sohoitis, you know . . . If you get Sohoitis, you will stay there always day and night and get no work done ever. You have been warned'.[31]

Pubs were of course not the only places offering alcohol and entertainment for night-time revellers. From around the turn of the century a growing number of clubs sprang up in Soho, initially providing meeting places for the foreigners in the population, and later increasingly catering for London's middle classes and intelligentsia. By 1913 Soho's clubs included the Cave of the Golden Calf, which had decorations by Wyndham Lewis and Jacob Epstein, and frequently staged a Galician gypsy floorshow. It was run by Frida Strindberg, and it quickly achieved notoriety:

> Down a dark cul-de-sac lurked a new and devilish sort of place where Futurists cavorted: a 'night club' profanely named 'The Cave of the Golden Calf' . . . the backstreets harboured all manner of such places, attended by members of the social elite . . . At the root of these evils lay the name of Oscar Wilde, still unspoken in polite households. He may have been dead for more than a decade, but Wilde's decadence endured.[32]

Meanwhile the Crabtree in Greek Street was opened by the painter Augustus John in April 1914, and quickly turned into a meeting place for bohemian artists, writers and poets. Walter Sickert and Jacob Epstein were among its clientele. Murray's in Beak Street reputedly introduced the tango to London around the same time. When Britain declared war on Germany in 1914, Augustus John told David Bomberg at the Café Royal, 'This is going to be bad for art'.[33]

The opposite was the case for Soho's illicit drinking clubs. Strict liquor laws led to the growth of illegal gambling, a 'cocaine epidemic', and drinking dens in Soho which outlived the war as many of the restrictions outlived it as well. The 'liberalisation' of wartime restrictions in 1921 allowed only nine hours of drinking on a weekday compared to the nineteen and a half before 1914. Some wryly wondered 'if, after all, we really did win the war', and many flocked to Soho, where clubs, drugs and sex became the dominant theme in the immediate post-war years.

This mixture led to an astonishing growth of Soho's clubs, live music and cabaret, attracting musicians from all over the world. 'All the famous coloured stars' performed at the Nest in Kingly Street, which also featured a cabaret with a one-legged tap dancer. The décor of some clubs became increasingly eccentric. Dalton Murray's Morgue Club in Ham Yard had a receptionist dressed as a nun, who apparently was 'far from virtuous', and the Blue Peter in Great Windmill Street was 'decked out like a battle ship'. The Gargoyle off Dean Street featured a rooftop dancefloor with Christmas trees in pots, and the Hell Club in Gerrard Street had 'hidden lighting that changed colour slowly, at a time when this was quite a novelty'.[34]

In 1921 Kate Meyrick founded the 43 Club in what had previously been the house of the poet John Dryden in Gerrard Street. After her marriage to a medical doctor had broken down in 1918, the Irishwoman took her six children to London and opened the 43 Club as the 'mother house' of her club empire. Her customers included the novelist Joseph Conrad, the sculptor Jacob Epstein and the writer J. B. Priestley. The 43's regulars included 'officers of distinguished regiments, members of the peerage, experienced Men about Town or rich young City magnates' who mixed with dancers, businessmen, delinquents and criminals.[35] The club increasingly attracted American musical talents such as Sophie Tucker and Paul Whiteman, which led to the 43 becoming a magnet for dance musicians working in the West End who had tired of playing bland hotel music. Meyrick recalled that Paul Whiteman 'would bring his band to play for us at the 43 after his theatre performance was over, and the mere rumour of his arrival was sufficient to crowd the club to the point of suffocation'.[36]

Meyrick's popularity with jazz musicians partly derived from the fact that she allowed them to perform improvisations, which were strictly prohibited in the elegant restaurants of the West

End. She aimed to create a transatlantic atmosphere in her club by encouraging her hostesses to use American slang or to acquire American accents, and by hosting jam sessions. She also installed a secret exit at the back of the club which proved ever more useful as the club gained in notoriety. It was frequently raided by the police, and Meyrick was charged on several occasions with selling alcohol without a licence and for out-of-hours drinking. Freda Kempton, a dance hostess of the club, died of a cocaine overdose after having last been seen at the club in company of 'Brilliant Chang', the Chinese restaurateur who was accused of providing her with drugs.

Her successful business ventures and her evident contempt for the law motivated Meyrick to fight against efforts to suppress London's nightclubs by puritanical home secretary Sir William Joynson-Hicks in the 1920s. She quickly became a heroine of the tabloid press due to her rebellious stance against drinking regulations. Her fame and wealth enabled her to send her children to elite schools, leading to the acquisition of several aristocratic son-in-laws. At a time when class distinctions were often still rigidly adhered to, the press observed that the relaxed atmosphere in her nightclubs led to strange alliances which broke with class lines and traditions.

Ultimately, however, the harsh conditions of London's prisons, where she was sent five times, ruined Meyrick's health and led to her untimely death aged fifty-seven in 1933. The 43 Club, which had quickly turned into the epitome of the illegal Soho club of the Roaring Twenties, was later used by Evelyn Waugh in his 1934 *A Handful of Dust* as inspiration for the Old Hundredth Club.

The 1930s also saw the rise of black clubs in Soho, drawing in both black and white patrons attracted by the jazz music of basement clubs. They included the Nest and Bag o' Nails in Kingly Street, the Blue Lagoon and Frisco's in Frith Street, as well as the Big Apple and Cuba Club in Gerrard Street. By the mid-1930s black clubs were advertised in entertainment guides – despite their often sleazy ambience, problems with gangland attacks and police raids.

Elegant people dining at The Blue Lagoon nightclub. Illustration by Dorothea St John George, in Horace Wyndham, *Nights in London: Where Mayfair Makes Merry*, 1926.

In 1937 the journalist Maurice Richardson commented that the only exception to the dull 'higher walks of nightlife' with its 'snooty boredom' were black clubs, where 'injections of negroes and swing have hotted up the night boxes'.[37]

The social mix in the black clubs included 'pale faces' from the suburbs jostling with prostitutes and pimps, single-sex dancing couples, lesbian waitresses who were visited by rich white women, international black stars, black working people and representatives of high bohemia. The Nest in Kingly Street and Jig's Club on Wardour Street were two of the most iconic black clubs of the period, where stars such as Louis Armstrong would socialise after their performances in West End theatres and cabarets. The Nest came to epitomise the Americanised nightclub spirit of 'peroxide hostesses, scruffy waiters, and "I have an uncle in the Mafia"'.[38]

The most famous of Soho's black clubs was Jack Isow's Shim Sham Club in Wardour Street, which attracted international celebrities and aristocracy such as Douglas Fairbanks and Lady Ashley. The jazz critic Leonard Feather described his visit in 1935 to what he called 'another London Harlem Club' with 'striking mural decorations' in an unexpectedly 'expansive and brilliantly lit room' with comfortable seating and a bandstand: 'Near beer, weeds, and lounge suits were the order of the night with many . . . Eight hours for work, eight hours for sleep, and eight hours at the Shim Sham. That will be the new daily round for these carefree coloured denizens of London.' *London Week* was also very enthusiastic, praising 'great hoofing, song and playing by such stars as Garland Wilson'.[39]

The Shim Sham also became something of a political space, attracting the radicals of Jewish London, socialists and communists. Musicians from ordinary backgrounds like Billy Amstell and Harry Gold, who played in elite nightclubs for London's wealthy, increasingly turned to socialism. Billy recalled: 'People used to come and they were well fed and they used to guzzle into their food and drink and only around the corner people were sleeping in doorways, wrapped in paper ... It reinforced my socialist convictions.'[40] Van Phillips of the Savoy Havana Band, and a major communist recruiter, commented that 'if you weren't a communist already, you'd be a bloody communist if you'd seen what we'd seen of the ruling class'.[41] Yet again Soho became a hotbed for political radicalism, with nightclubs such as the Shim Sham attracting anti-fascists, socialists, communists and audiences of a broad racial diversity, as well as a cross-section of society.

The strict post-war licensing laws led to ever more attempts to find ways to drink late into the night, and Soho was at the heart of the emerging 'bottle party craze' of the late 1920s and 1930s. Originating with the Bright Young Things of the 1920s for their own private parties, bottle parties then became part of the Soho club scene. Ostensibly there by invitation, club-goers ordered drink in advance with a wine merchant, thereby using the nightclub for a private party. As these events were private, they were exempt from the licensing laws, but in reality anyone could gain entrance to these parties by paying a fee at the door. In 1935 the police estimated there were at least fifty bottle parties in the Soho area, and *What's On* announced in 1937 that 'Night clubs are no more. These days the private party has taken their place'.[42]

The Second World War led to an increasingly hectic nightlife in Soho's clubs and bars. Off-duty gay officers often drank the night away at the Café Royal, also a favourite of Dylan Thomas's. When this closed, revellers moved on to drinking clubs such as the Horseshoe in Wardour Street or the Byron in Greek Street. The increasing number of Black American GIs in London often danced the night away with local girls in music clubs such as the Sunset and Moonglow – and there was, of course, the ill-fated Café de Paris. In 1924 the Rialto cinema at Nos 3–4 Coventry Street had been built, with a large underground restaurant that was converted into a nightclub, the Café de Paris. Its interior was based on the Palm Court of the luxury liner SS *Lusitania*, and in its heyday during the inter-war period it operated as a supper club open to the elites of society, frequented by royals such as the kings of Greece, Spain, Norway and Portugal and Edward, the Prince of Wales. Its cabaret featured stars such as Marlene Dietrich and Maurice Chevalier.

On the night of 8 March 1941 the basement bar of the Café de Paris was crowded with revellers, despite the Blitz, as the deep-level club was advertised as 'the safest place to dance in town'. Off-duty officers and London society people were enjoying the sound of Ken 'Snakehips' Johnson's band, the West Indian Dance Orchestra. Ken Johnson, a handsome Guyanese dancer well over 6 feet tall, had developed his signature hip-swivelling dance based on the technique used by the American dancer Earl 'Snakehips' Tucker, and his band was the first in London to gain bookings in elite West End clubs such as Mayfair's Florida Club and the Café de Paris.

Johnson had spent the early part of the evening at the Embassy Club in Mayfair but, not wanting to let the management of the Café de Paris down, he ran through the blackout and arrived at 9.45pm, just in time for his band to go on stage. Their first song led to many revellers crowding on to the dance floor, but only minutes into 'Oh Johnny!' two high explosive bombs hit the Rialto cinema above the club, and crashed down into the Café de Paris. The devastating blast killed many people, including Snakehips Johnson. Thirty-four bodies were recovered from the wreckage, but the death toll later rose to over eighty. Many people had their clothes torn off them, and survivors, reeling in shock, stumbled out into the street covered in dust and plaster. Yorke de Souza, the Jamaican pianist of Johnson's band, was among the survivors. He had £60 on him when the disaster happened but when he got home the money was gone, probably 'taken from me by the looters'. Looters also 'took the cufflinks from the manager's corpse'.[43]

The Café de Paris reopened in 1948, once again becoming London's most glamorous nightclub, and on many occasions hosted Princess Margaret and her circle. However, its demise came with the advent of the Swinging Sixties and the decline of

Emergency workers clear out the bomb-damaged interior of the Café de Paris, 9 March 1941.

traditional 'society', leading to the club's transformation into a mere dance venue.

After the Second World War the best jazz music could still be heard in Soho, often in tiny little basements that had been converted, with self-avowed grandness, into clubs. The tradition of after-hours drinking clubs also continued unabated in the area. The Mandrake in Meard Street was one of the most popular venues for Soho's bohemia just after the war. It started as a chess club, but in order to make enough money a bar was installed which meant that very quickly the place was taken over by drinkers and the drunks. To circumvent licensing laws, alcohol could only be served with food outside pub hours. A collection of dry sandwiches was therefore kept behind the bar, and whenever a customer complained about the state of them the owner would explain that 'this is a sandwich for drinking with, not for eating!'[44]

The Colony Room Club in Dean Street – or Muriel's, as it became known, 'for the energy and humour dispensed by the charismatic bisexual from Birmingham'[45] – was simply a bar in a small room, and became one of the favourite drinking dens of Soho's artists and writers. It opened around 1948 or 1949, and its 700 members included Francis Bacon, Lucian Freud and, until her alcohol-induced incontinence began to ruin the bar stools, the artist and writer Nina Hamnett. Muriel's opened from three in the afternoon to eleven at night, thereby enabling its customers to bridge the gap caused by licensing laws that forced all other Soho clubs to stay closed until 5.30pm.

When Muriel's closed at 11pm its customers would simply move across the street to the lavishly decorated Gargoyle Club, to dance through the night. The next morning the York Minster pub served pastis as a hangover cure and – for those whose liver and wallet could take it – pre-lunch drinks (eating food was not actually a requirement) which then turned into oysters and champagne at Wheeler's before the party returned to Muriel's. Many of Soho's artists and writers hopped on and off this 'merry-go-round lifestyle', depending on how many of their paintings or books they managed to sell. However, as writer Sophie Parkin ruminates, 'Who lived this kind of life apart from Bacon? Not many'.[46]

Muriel's was seen as the smaller, more homosexually tolerant version of its neighbour, the Gargoyle Club. The Gargoyle was a nightclub in the traditional sense, offering a dining area, a dance band and a cocktail bar. The design featured a red glass interior by Matisse and décor by Lutyens, and the club had a lift to get to the fifth floor. It was established by the socialite the Hon. David Pax Tennant and his actress wife Hermione Baddeley, who often appeared at the Gargoyle in cabaret. The club's clientele included Noël Coward, Francis Bacon and Dylan Thomas, and many of its members were also frequent guests at Muriel's. Opposite the Gargoyle and next door to Muriel's was the Caves de France, which in many ways was the antithesis to Muriel's, as customers tended to patronise either the one or the other. The club promoted itself as a 'social club for French-speaking people and meeting place for poets, painters, writers and artists'.[47]

A new kind of Soho club emerged in 1949, when Ronnie Scott and a group of musicians founded Club 41 in Archer Street. It was devoted to bebop, the latest form of jazz music. It moved to Carnaby Street in 1950, but was shut down shortly afterwards due to a drugs raid. At Scott's trial the magistrate famously asked 'What is bebop?', to which the Chief Inspector replied, 'It is a queer form of modern dancing – a Negro jive'.[48]

For many visitors to post-war Soho, the area became synonymous with the porn trade and the Raymond Revuebar. Opened in a seedy alleyway in Walker's Court, the bar turned Paul Raymond into the uncrowned king of Soho's porn industry and the sex business's 'Mr Clean'. According to the American journalist Piri Halasz, who penned the famous 1966 *Time* article on Swinging London, the Raymond Revuebar 'is the most famous and the most reliable of the Soho strip houses. Expensive and crowded . . . The biggest attraction recently has been an Australian blonde named Rita Elen who gets knocked about by

Paul Raymond with dancers from the Raymond Revuebar, 1988.

a hirsute rich man's Johnny Weissmuller with a whip while she does an exotic dance with a fully grown live cheetah'.[49]

At the height of Swinging London it was Soho's sex industry that attracted a certain clientele, consisting, to quote Halasz again, mostly of 'Midlands business men, rag-trade tycoons, jockeys, slumlords or unhip American tourists' to the area:

> London takes on a special gloss at night, but it is the darkness that creates it, not the neon lights. The unsophisticated American traveller gravitates towards Soho or Leicester Square to leer at the strip houses and the pornographic bookstores and cinemas, eye the women in the street whom he hopes are prostitutes, or palm his dollars in the monster cabarets. Then he concludes that London nightlife is flashy, sleazy, sexy, second-rate and wide-open.[50]

In the eyes of Halasz this gave Soho 'the distinction of being outstandingly sad and sleazy, tawdry, teasing, cynical and vulgar'. A *Swinger's Guide to London* concluded that a list of places where 'no swinger would be caught dead' included 'Raymond's Revue Bar, the Pigalle, or the Black and White Minstrel Show'.[51]

Endless Nights

From the mid-nineteenth century onwards, Soho increasingly developed into London's prime location for restaurants, cafés, pubs, bars, clubs and erotic entertainment. The eclectic mixture of people attracted by the area made Soho successful. Poor working-class Londoners mixed with members of royalty and high society. International film and music stars, comedians, artists, writers and bohemians were attracted to Soho's air of excitement, cosmopolitanism and the fact that many things considered illegal or morally reprehensible were perfectly acceptable in Soho.

This attraction continued throughout the twentieth century, as Piri Halasz discovered on her visits to Soho: 'If you really want a wild crowd, there are obvious places to go looking for one: in the cheapest Soho discotheques, which are little more than pickup joints, the beat pubs nearby, or the shadiest jazz clubs.' She described Soho's discotheques and jazz clubs as places 'to watch the beats, aspiring pop musicians, their agents, the Indians and West Indians who form an essential cog in the wheels of the contemporary pop scene, together with all the young kids who don't have a bean but are still full of beans'.[52]

The dives and pubs of Soho came increasingly to represent the centre of cultural change, not only in London, but in all of Britain. Soho had already become an artistic bohemia by the late 1930s, attracting literary figures such as Dylan Thomas. The basement clubs that sprang up in the 1920s had multiplied by the 1950s, and now offered jazz, beat and later skiffle music to London's post-war youth.

In the 1960s the area yet again rose to international fame as Soho (together with Chelsea) became the epicentre of a youth culture. As the historian Roy Porter writes of this period, 'there was a rare alliance between youth culture and commerce, aristocratic style and new populism. It was a breath of fresh air'. He continues:

for a while [the area] was remarkably successful in bringing together artists, art-school students, the radical intelligentsia and the young, but also go-ahead men and women in fashion, music, advertising, design, publicity, publishing, film, television, the media. A culture materialised that was irreverent, offbeat, creative, novel. Politically idealistic and undogmatically left-wing, it broke through class barriers and captured and transformed many of the better elements of traditional London: its cosmopolitanism and openness, its village quality, its closeness, its cocktail of talent, wealth and eccentricity.[53]

Soho's world of entertainment brought the area to the attention of the world. But of course this world was made up of the unique mix of people who either lived in or frequented Soho. It was the musicians, actors, film stars, bohemians, royals and jet setters who increasingly made Soho the focus of the world's media. It was the restaurateurs, waiters, theatre staff, publicans and barmaids, among many others, who were the source of the area's continued success. And it was of course the prostitutes, pimps and members of the underworld who provided the area with an air of danger, sleaze and excitement.

It is therefore now time to look at the people who, throughout Soho's history, have contributed to its unique character. The next chapter looks at Soho's citizens alongside the rich and famous who made Soho their spiritual home.

'Soho.' Photograph by Francis Sandwith, from *London by Night*, 1935..

Chapter 5 **Women and Men of Soho**

'Soho in the fifties? That wasn't our Soho. It had nothing to do with the local residents. We weren't remotely involved.'[1] As this statement by a life-long resident of Berwick Street highlights, there was a long-held tradition for many ordinary members of Soho's communities to largely ignore the often famous and wealthy artists, writers, musicians and radicals who invaded their district.

It was partly the cosmopolitan nature of the communities that attracted the bohemians, revolutionaries, socialites and tourists, and many Soho residents arguably benefited financially from the fame that these celebrities brought to the area. Social and sexual behaviour that was condemned in all other parts of the capital was generally accepted by the people of Soho. The area attracted a wide range of escapees from all walks of life who, although few of them actually lived in Soho, gave the area its unique character and reputation.

This chapter looks firstly at the communities of ordinary Sohoites, their backgrounds and lives as well as their decline in numbers over the years, and secondly at some of those women and men who made the place their spiritual home and frequented its many bars, restaurants and brothels. The wide range of foreign influences shaped the communities of the area and some of these are looked at here, before exploring the lives of some of the actors, writers, artists, film stars and bohemians who left their mark on the area.

The Communities

The population of Soho underwent dramatic changes in terms of its size within a time of only 100 years. A district of working-class communities with desperate levels of overcrowding, poverty and disease – where in the 1860s 'dwellings that originally sheltered eight or ten persons are now crowded with thirty, forty, or fifty inmates'[2] – was transformed into an area largely dominated by leisure, retail and business only a century later. Although in the 1950s the Soho of Colin MacInnes' *Absolute Beginners* was still the scene of 'dear old Italians and sweet old Viennese who've run their honest, unbent little businesses there since the days of George six, and five, and backward far beyond', fewer and fewer of them actually lived in the area.[3]

This exodus of ordinary Sohoites in the middle of the twentieth century was largely caused by changes dating back to the Victorian era. Soho's fortunes were transformed towards the end of the nineteenth century by the dramatic development of leisure, commerce and transportation, the effects of which are still visible to this day. The creation of streets such as Regent Street, Shaftesbury Avenue and Charing Cross Road opened up Soho to commercial and industrial opportunities, and cemented Soho's modern identity. By the early twentieth century the streets of Soho were accessible to unprecedented numbers of people from London, as well as further afield, via the electrified underground railway.

It was this new accessibility – combined with post Second World War affluence, consumerism and the birth of the teenager – which turned the streets of Soho into the epicentre of London's Swinging Sixties. However, these developments and the accompanying commercialisation of Soho were also a key cause of the rapid decline of the number of working-class residents. This decline began as early as the 1860s in some areas, and 100 years later Soho was described as 'essentially a place of business: there are Clubs, Bookshops, Film Distributors,

'Absinthe Drinkers.' Plate from G. R. Sims (ed.), *Living London. Its Work and its Play. Its Humour and its Pathos. Its Sights and its Scenes*, Cassell 1901.

Strip Joints, Clip Joints, Pubs, Gambling Rooms and especially Restaurants'.[4] Soho's population had declined from 24,000 in 1900 to 7,240 in 1939.

The cosmopolitan character of Soho that emerged in the nineteenth century quickly transformed the neighbourhood, and even when London overall became less multicultural in the inter-war period, due to stricter immigration laws, the opposite was true for Soho. An Armenian café emerged in Great Windmill Street, and in his impressions of London life in 1915 the author Thomas Burke commented on the large numbers of Spanish, Chinese, Indian, Hungarian, Greek and Jewish restaurants in Soho.[5] Immigrants from Sweden, Norway and Denmark left their mark, and were often employed in the tailoring and shoemaking industries. At the turn of the century there were also more than 250 Swiss living in Soho.

There had long been a strong French flavour in Soho, due to the history of French settlement dating back to the seventeenth century, and also due to the determination of the community to retain its French culture, language and character. As individual French migrants often returned to France after a stint in London, it was quite rare to find a second generation of French residents in the area. The community arguably made few attempts to assimilate. Many of Soho's shops were French, selling French goods such as wooden shoes and berets. Alongside the many French restaurants were pubs, cafés and hotels.

Although the area retained a French flavour throughout the nineteenth century, German and Italian culture, music and cuisine were added to the existing offerings. The Germans made up by far the largest minority in London at the turn of the century. From the 1860s many of them left their East End trades like sugar baking, boot making and cigar making to settle in places like Soho instead, to join the restaurant and service trades as well as tailoring. Both in the 'Charlottenstrasse' area north of Oxford Street and in Soho many German hotels, restaurants and shops opened, while German social clubs (*Vereine*) became a distinct feature of Soho.

The German Workers' Education Society established itself in Great Windmill Street and here, at the Red Lion pub, Karl Marx and Friedrich Engels submitted their proposals for writing *The Communist Manifesto* in 1848. Prior to the First World War a German Military Union regularly met in Wardour Street. The fact that the majority of German immigrants were men meant that, due to their intermarriage with English women, they tended to be the most assimilated of all of London's minorities and therefore not as much in the public eye as, for example, their Italian counterparts.

The migration of London's Italian communities into Soho towards the end of the nineteenth century was partly due to the growing popularity of ice cream. First sold in London in the summer of 1850, the business was firmly in the hands of the Italian communities and constituted their first step towards the catering industry and the opening of Italian restaurants in Soho. The arrival of the catering trade also brought Italian anarchists towards the end of the nineteenth century, who used Soho as a base to produce propaganda for export to the continent. They were also a driving force leading to the establishment of the Caterer Workers Union, and Soho was a centre of Italian anarchist clubs, restaurants and meeting places. Soho anarchists such as shopkeeper Emidio Recchioni, decorator Pietro Guadacci and compositor Silvio Corio had come to Soho to join forces with the exiled anarchist Errico Malatesta, who resided in North London. Malatesta supported violent insurrection, political assassination and forcible redistribution of wealth but, like most Italian anarchists in Britain, he kept a low profile and did not break the law so as to avoid deportation.

Soho's Italian population had begun to grow before the First World War, but it grew considerably more so afterwards. By 1934 Soho could be described as the Italian quarter of London – one writer pointed out in the 1930s that the headquarters of 'their very active Fascism' was located in Greek Street.[6] The Italian leader Benito Mussolini was keen to transform London into a

Eugenio Celoria making tagliatelli in his shop, King Bomba's. Photograph by Felix Man, published in *Picture Post*, 25 March 1939.

prime example of an Italian fascist colony; the London Fascio, established in Noel Street in Soho in 1921, was the first to be organised outside of Italy. According to the historian Terri Colpi, Soho's Italians were to be transformed into 'Mussolini's greatest fans and propagandists',[7] and they enjoyed the full support of the Catholic Church, including the local parish priest of Soho. A number of prominent Sohoites such as Pepino Leoni, the owner of the famous Quo Vadis restaurant on Dean Street, supported the regime. Many Italian Sohoites therefore had divided loyalties, having both an allegiance to the Fascist regime as well as respect for the laws and institutions of Britain.

However, not all the Italian inhabitants of Soho supported Mussolini. The aforementioned anarchist Emidio Recchioni used the profits he made from his shop, King Bomba on Old Compton Street, to help finance two failed assassination attempts on the Duce. Recchioni's shop became a meeting point for anti-Fascists, including intellectuals such as Sylvia Pankhurst, George Orwell and Emma Goldman.

When Mussolini declared war on Britain in 1940, Soho's Italians were suddenly condemned as enemy aliens. Soho became the focus of an eruption of anti-Italian sentiment in the 'Battle of Soho', when hostile crowds descended on the area and many Italian premises were looted. Many men of Italian origin were arrested and interned, despite the fact that they often had spent most of their lives in Soho. Nearly 500 of them died when SS *Arandora Star*, a ship carrying enemy aliens to Canada, was sunk by a German submarine.

Thus, the fortunes of the immigrant communities of Soho were closely tied to the outbreak of war in 1914 and 1939. The fate of both Italian and German immigrants of Soho was to take dramatic turns with anti-German riots after the outbreak of the Great War in 1914 and the indiscriminate internment of Londoners of Italian descent in 1940. Neither community fully recovered from the impact of the two wars.

A further victim of the war, if for very different reasons, was the Jewish community of Soho. Traditionally the Jewish population of London resided in the East End. However, by the mid-eighteenth century Jewish residents increasingly also lived in West London, most notably in Rupert Street, Broad Street, Carnaby Street, Great Windmill Street and Berwick Street in Soho. From the 1850s onwards the story of the Jewish community in Soho was one of 'self-help in which respect for heritage and identity was balanced with successful integration into British society'.[8] By the 1850s a Western Jewish Girls' Free School had been established at No. 6 Greek Street. Most Jews settling in Soho from the 1880s onwards came from Eastern Europe, but numbers also increased because, as was explained in a 1911 history of the area, 'the tailors' strike in 1891 was the cause of a considerable exodus of Israelites from Whitechapel to Soho'.[9] Many worked as domestic servants, but the majority were employed in the garment trade, producing dresses, caps and waistcoats, often supplying the upmarket tailors of Savile Row on the other side of Regent Street.

As Jewish immigration rose at a time when the overall population of Soho was falling, the predominance of the Jewish community grew significantly. In 1900 approximately 40 per cent of the inhabitants of St Anne's Parish was Jewish. When only 4 per cent of London's population was foreign-born, 6,000 out of 13,000 residents in Soho were Jewish, and it was an even higher percentage around Berwick Street. Victorian social reformer Charles Booth commented that the Jewish immigrants 'make a street look bad, but their influence has been quieting to the district'.[10] Many of the Jewish residents of Soho were better off than those of the East End, and according to the above-mentioned 1911 history of the area, 'prosperity is usually written upon their faces'.[11] Of course Soho appeared to have the same effect on many of the Jewish residents as it had on others – Chief Rabbi Hermann Adler complained in 1897 that 'the West Enders of Soho were surrounded by crowded

'A Concert at the Jewish Working Girls' Club, Soho.' Plate in G. R. Sims (ed.), *Living London. Its Work and its Play. Its Humour and its Pathos. Its Sights and its Scenes*, Cassell 1901.

streets full of snares and pitfalls, and they had the reputation of being generally irreligious'.[12]

Soho's Jewish population began to decline in the twentieth century for the same reasons the overall population of Central London had been falling since the early 1900s. Push factors such as rising rents due to commercialisation and the growth of office employment played an important part; pull factors included the rise of suburbanisation, increasing affluence, and the desire for more space and better housing. People moved to places such as Highgate, Cricklewood and Golders Green; those who remained mostly had their businesses in the West End. This exodus of the Jewish community was particularly exacerbated by the Blitz. One resident remembered, 'I think the bombs that landed in 1941 heralded the end of an era of the vibrant Jewish community in the West End'.[13]

Women and Men of Soho

Even prior to its rise to fame, the overcrowded streets of poverty-stricken mid-nineteenth-century Soho were home to famous residents such as Karl Marx and the physician John Snow. Snow had been educated at the Great Windmill Street School of Medicine in the 1830s, and set up his practice on Frith Street thereafter. He became one of Britain's first specialist anaesthetists, and it was his ground-breaking research during the cholera outbreak of 1854 in Soho that convinced him that the disease was not caused by miasma but was a waterborne disease. He produced a detailed map of the area around the Broad Street water pump in Soho, charting where the hundreds of victims lived. The evidence clearly pointed towards the pump as the source of the disease, but his findings were not accepted by the medical profession until after his premature death.

While Soho's population declined in numbers over time, its status as an entertainment centre grew, which led to an ever

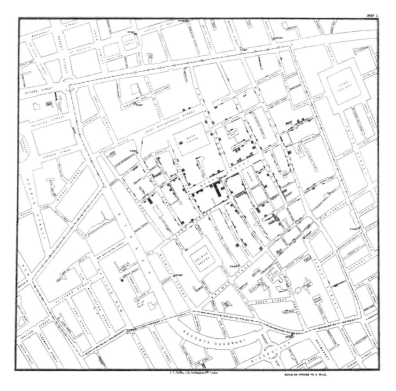

Snow's spot map of the Golden Square outbreak, from *Report of the Cholera Outbreak in the Parish of St. James, Westminster during the Autumn of 1854. Presented to the Vestry by the Cholera Inquiry Committee, July 1855.*

increasing number of famous actors, musicians, artists and writers from Britain and around the world spending their time in Soho and thereby adding to the distinctive character of the area. Politicians, journalists and other celebrities joined them in the many bars, restaurants and clubs. Soho's position at the heart of London's West End made it an ideal playground for bohemians.

Many of Britain's most famous actors, some of whom were Soho residents, performed in the West End's theatres, and their paths often crossed in Soho.

The theatrical genius Edmund Kean – who at the height of his fame, 'drink-sodden and suffering from venereal disease', enjoyed parading his pet lion in the streets of London – had been abandoned by his mother in a doorway in Frith Street and was brought up by an uncle in Lisle Street.[14] His son Charles Kean, actor, stage manager and 'truly a Victorian gentleman', ran the Princess's theatre on Oxford Street, which was London's leading theatre from 1850 until 1859.[15] Fanny Kelly played Ophelia to Edmund Kean's Hamlet at the newly rebuilt Theatre Royal, Drury Lane. She later lived at 73 Dean Street, where she opened her financially disastrous theatre. Later, the theatre impresario and born-and-bred Sohoite Richard D'Oyly Carte would stage the first Gilbert and Sullivan operetta, *Trial by Jury*, there. William Charles Macready, who had been pallbearer at Edmund Kean's funeral and is above all remembered for his performances in Shakespeare's tragedies, recalled visiting Miss Kelly's theatre and enjoying a farce performed by Charles Dickens, which he thought 'very broad and laughable'.[16]

Nelly Moore, who came to fame as the original Ada Ingot in T. W. Robertson's *David Garrick* at the Theatre Royal, Haymarket, died of typhoid fever at 31 Soho Square at the age of only twenty-four. Fanny Kemble, actress and author, was born in Newham Street, just north of Soho, and her father Charles Kemble, 'unrivalled in the legitimate comic repertory', had always been enamoured by Soho and had lived at both Gerrard Street and Soho Square.[17] Sir Henry Irving, the first British actor ever to be knighted, made

STRICTLY PRIVATE.

MISS KELLY'S THEATRE,

No. 73, DEAN STREET, SOHO SQUARE.

MISS KELLY HAS THE HONOR TO ANNOUNCE TO THE NOBILITY, GENTRY, HER SUBSCRIBERS, AND FRIENDS,

THAT HER BENEFIT IS FIXED FOR

SATURDAY, JANUARY the 3rd., 1846,

UPON WHICH OCCASION THE

DISTINGUISHED AMATEURS

Whose Performances have created such extraordinary interest, and confirmed the still existing taste for the legitimate Drama, will (as a tribute of regard for which she cannot express too much her gratified feelings and deep sense of obligation) appear for the last time.

THE PERFORMANCES WILL CONSIST OF (ALTERED FOR THIS REPRESENTATION)

ELETCHER'S COMEDY OF

THE ELDER BROTHER.

CHARACTERS IN THE PLAY.

LOUIS	(A Lord)		Mr. DUDLEY COSTELLO
MIRAMONT			Mr. MARK LEMON.
BRISAC	A Justice, } Country Brother to } Gentlemen Miramont }		Mr. LEECH.
CHARLES	(a Scholar)	} Sons to {	Mr. FORSTER.
EUSTACE	(a Courtier)	} Brisac {	Mr. CHARLES DICKENS.
EGREMONT	} Friends to		Mr. FREDERICK DICKENS.
COWSY	} Eustace		Mr. AUGUSTUS DICKENS.
NOTARY			Mr. W. H. WILLS.
ANDREW	(Servant to Charles)		Mr. DOUGLAS JERROLD.
	Cook, Butler, &c. &c.		
ANGELINA	} Daughter to {		Miss FORTESCUE.
	} Louis {		
SYLVIA	(her Woman)		Miss HINTON.

A Prologue will be spoken by Miss KELLY.

AND

MR. PEAKE'S FARCE OF

COMFORTABLE LODGINGS.

CAPTAIN BONASSUS (an old French Officer)		Mr. FRANK STONE.
BOMBADIER BABILLARD (his comrade)		Mr. LEECH.
VINCENT DORVILLE (Lover of Antoinette)		Mr. AUGUSTUS DICKENS.
SIR FLIPPINGTON MIFF (an English Traveller)		Mr. CHARLES DICKENS.
RIGMAROLE (his Valet)		Mr. MARK LEMON.
ROUÉ (a broken Lieutenant)		Mr. GEORGE CRUIKSHANK.
MONSIEUR DE CACHET (Intendant of French Police)		Mr. FORSTER.
GREGORY (Servant to Bonassus)		Mr. W. H. WILLS.
ANTOINETTE (Daughter to Bonassus)		Miss MAY.
MADAM PELAGIE (Sister to Bonassus)		Miss BEW.

Play bill for Miss Kelly's Theatre, 3 January 1846. Charles Dickens is listed among the 'distinguished amateurs' performing this comic double bill, playing the role of Eustace, a courtier, in *The Elder Brother*, and Sir Flippington Miff in *Comfortable Lodgings*.

his first stage appearance at the Soho Theatre. After a long acting career Irving managed the Lyceum theatre from 1878 onwards, and turned it into what one critic called 'the embodiment of all that is refined, sumptuous and noble in English histrionic art'.[18] Irving's manager of business was Bram Stoker, now famous to us as the author of *Dracula*. Under Stoker's management the Lyceum theatre offered such entertainment as transforming the stage into a pavilion after performances and serving guests unlimited lobster, chicken and champagne. Together Irving and Stoker transformed the Lyceum into the cultural heart of London. Irving was also the inspiration for the 'physical characteristics and mesmerising personality' of Stoker's Dracula.[19]

Irving found his soulmate in the young actress Ellen Terry, whose beauty made her as much an art object as an actress. She became a muse for many poets and painters of the age, including the Pre-Raphaelites and Oscar Wilde. She worked closely with Irving for twenty-four years. Their close association probably also involved a sexual relationship – both were in unhappy marriages. A portrait of the actress by her first husband, George Frederic Watts, now hangs in the National Portrait Gallery. There is a statue near the National Portrait Gallery commemorating Irving, who died in 1905. It stands on what may well have been the site of Charles Dickens's Old Curiosity Shop.

The actor William Terriss, after a brief spell working with Irving, came to fame at the Adelphi theatre where 'his muscularity in swashbuckling hero parts' gained him the nickname 'No. 1 Adelphi Terriss'. He was sensationally murdered at his own stage door when an actor he had just sacked stabbed him in the back in 1897.

A former actor held in high regard by Henry Irving was theatrical wigmaker Willy Clarkson – Irving laid the coping stone for Clarkson's business in Wardour Street. His appearance was eccentric. His friend, the lawyer William Charles Crocker, recalled that Clarkson's hair was 'dyed a near chest-nut . . . curled poetically', and his 'heavy moustache, like the horns of a cow, turned up a little at either end' and 'his chubby cheeks . . . lightly touched with rouge'. Clarkson 'cast himself as the artistic simpleton, a businessman, *malgré lui* of whose coy, languishing innocence, everybody, *just everybody*, took advantage'.[20] This was a shrewd and clever disguise, as not only did his business thrive and supply wigs for most of London's theatres for nearly fifty years, but Clarkson was also an accomplished insurance fraudster, with most of the buildings he occupied succumbing to fires. He was also a notorious blackmailer.

Soho's association with the world of actors continued unabated in the twentieth century. The delicate-looking Billie Carleton played her first major role in the 1914 Empire Theatre revue *Watch your Step*. Her looks and talent quickly propelled her to stardom, and she became the youngest leading lady in the West End. What followed was a life of glamour, luxury – and drug use. Her untimely death in her Savoy suite after the Victory Ball at the Albert Hall in November 1918 from a drug overdose made drug abuse front-page news. Noël Coward used her story as inspiration for *The Vortex*, and the association of the opium trade with London's Chinatown (as well as Carleton's romantic involvement with at least three wealthy men) transformed her into 'a symbol of the drug-threatened and wronged female abused by older, usually foreign, men'.[21]

In 1938 John Gielgud starred in and directed Oscar Wilde's *The Importance of Being Earnest* in the theatre which today bears his name, then named the Globe Theatre, on the corner of Rupert Street and Shaftesbury Avenue. Here Noël Coward's play *Fallen Angels* also debuted in 1925. Jessie Matthews, one of eleven children of a Berwick Street Market trader, was born in Soho in 1907. She made her first stage appearance as a dancer at the age of twelve in London, and her New York debut at the age of just sixteen. In 1928 she starred in Noël Coward's *This Year of Grace* to critical acclaim and, having reached the peak of her theatrical career, became Britain's first international

 011795 l. 65

Front cover of programme for *Watch Your Step* at the Empire Theatre, 1914.

film star. She starred in fourteen films in the 1930s, including *The Good Companions* (1933) opposite John Gielgud. Ironically her own musical production *I Can Take It* was cancelled due to the outbreak of war in 1939. Despite personal tragedies, her film and television career revived after the Second World War and she appeared frequently both on screen and on stage until shortly before her death in 1981.

Soho also served as inspiration and haven for many of Britain's most famous writers. Apart from appearing on stage at the Soho Theatre, Charles Dickens – described by Thomas Carlyle as the 'quiet, shrewd-looking, little fellow'[22] – also used Soho as the home for several of his fictional characters. Ralph Nickleby lives in Soho Square, while the lawyer Mr Jaggers of *Great Expectations* has his offices in Gerrard Street, in 'a stately house of its kind but dolefully in want of painting'. Thomas De Quincey's famous *Confessions of an English Opium Eater* contained a vivid account of his relationship with 'Anne of Oxford Street', a young prostitute who, when he fainted from hunger in Soho Square, spent her last money on wine to revive him.

From a well-to-do background and well-educated, De Qunicey nonetheless broke off relations with his family and ran away to Soho at the age of seventeen, where he slept in an unfurnished house in Greek Street. Despite frantic searching he never saw Anne again, but the impression she made on him remained with him for the rest of his life. Also lifelong was the opium addiction that he developed after trying to cure a toothache with laudanum to soothe the pain. Later he took opium simply due to the 'abyss of divine enjoyment . . . suddenly revealed' by ingestion of the drug.[23]

One of the most famous writers intimately associated with Soho was Oscar Wilde who, prior to his trial and imprisonment in 1895 for his homosexual affairs, frequently lunched at the Café Royal, often dined at Kettner's in Romilly Street, and met male prostitutes at an address in Rupert Street. After a varied and increasingly successful career as writer, lecturer and dandy

Photographic portrait of Oscar Wilde, from *The Cabinet Portrait Gallery. Photographs by W. & D. Downey*, 1890–94.

had taken him to Paris and the United States, Wilde settled in London where he married Constance Lloyd and their two sons were born. It was here that his career as writer and playwright brought him fame, culminating in the success of his final play, *The Importance of Being Earnest*, in 1895.

It was the world of the West End's theatres which, for Wilde, provided 'a haven where homosexuality found acknowledgement, if not acceptance. It also meant that enemies could discover more, quicker'.[24] The ruin of his own and his family's personal lives, the tarnishing of his reputation and the loss of his home and possessions, including even his children's toys, combined with the destructive experience of imprisonment after his trial, serve as a reminder of how so many of London's private pleasures lived out in Soho's underworld were still deemed utterly unacceptable by society at large in late Victorian London.

While staying in Paris in 1883 Wilde met Paul Verlaine, the French Symbolist poet who, after his involvement in the 1871 Paris Commune, left his wife and child to start a short and torrid love affair with Arthur Rimbaud. This led the pair to stay in London and frequent the bars of Soho in 1872. Another notable member of Soho's literary circle was Joseph Conrad, who settled in England in 1894 after spending twenty years at sea as master mariner of the British merchant navy. Born Józef Teodor Konrad Korzeniowski, of Polish descent, he used many of his voyages as material for his later writings, and published his first novel at the age of thirty-eight. He quickly established a reputation for exotic and adventurous fiction, and ultimately became arguably Britain's greatest political novelist. His masterpiece was *Heart of Darkness*, based on one of his journeys through the Congo Free State in 1890, when he travelled overland and in a paddle-steamer. Conrad's literary friends included H. G. Wells, John Galsworthy and Ford Madox Ford, and he regularly met fellow writers at the Mont Blanc restaurant on Gerrard Street as well as occasionally visiting the 43 Club. His 1907 work *The Secret*

Agent features the villain Verloc, who manages a pornographic bookshop in Soho.

Virginia Woolf was a frequent visitor to the area during the inter-war period, and she enjoyed the vibrancy of Soho. Her husband Leonard had been co-founder of the 1917 Club, a socialist establishment in Gerrard Street, and although they did not join those of their fellow club members who went across the road to have an illicit drink at Mrs Meyrick's infamous 43 Club, Virginia and Leonard frequently met friends in Soho's restaurants. Virginia Woolf browsed the stalls of Charing Cross Road bookshops, and often haggled with the traders of Berwick Street Market. Soho provided her with inspiration for her 1922 novel *Jacob's Room*, which was one of her first steps towards redefining fiction throughout the inter-war period and was 'almost ostentatiously modern'.[25]

In the late 1980s Daniel Farson's book *Soho in the Fifties* was a huge success. His position as a photographer at *Picture Post* brought him to 1950s Soho, where he took many memorable photographs of his friends, who included Francis Bacon, John Deakin and Lucian Freud. His most famous shots include that of Gaston Berlemont opening a bottle for his patrons at the French pub, and a hung-over Jeffrey Bernard in Soho Square. Losing his job at *Picture Post*, he joined the merchant navy. On returning to London he became a celebrity television presenter, known especially for a series of unconventional documentaries on topics such as witchcraft and interracial marriages. He became a recluse in later life, only occasionally returning to Soho for casual homosexual sex, drunken excess and the odd moment of violence.

Soho also featured heavily in the 1950s London of Colin MacInnes. His mother was the novelist Angela Margaret Thirkell. They shared a mutual loathing for each other – she cut him out of her will, and he chose some of the themes of his work because he knew his mother would be disgusted by them:

'drugs, prostitution, race riots, and the teenage revolution' were the most prominent features of the trilogy of his London novels, and he was the writer most in touch with the young generation of musicians, who 'have organised their underground of joy'.[26] Being openly homosexual at a time when this was still illegal, he often drank at the French pub and Muriel's Colony Room Club with friends such as the musician George Melly.

Soho's association with musicians predates the nineteenth century – the young Mozart performed concerts during his stay in London at 21 Dean Street in 1764. Richard Wagner spent some time at a hotel in Old Compton Street during his first stay in London, later returning to Soho in the 1870s to retrace the steps of that first visit. From 1871 to 1886 the composer and conductor Sir Joseph Barnby was organist and choirmaster of St Anne's in Dean Street. Here his musical services were performed by his choir of sixty-four (which included thirty-two boy trebles), who attended choir practice with him every day. The services turned into a popular attraction, drawing in large crowds, and quickly gained the nickname the 'Sunday opera'.

One unusual musician living in Golden Square was Vladimir de Pachmann, the famous pianist known for his performances of Chopin. He was well known for his eccentric style of performance, which often included gestures and muttering, as well as talking to the audience. His bizarre behaviour involved demanding that ugly people be removed from the front rows during his performances, and inviting fellow pianists from the audience to play on stage. It was probably this behaviour that earned him the nickname 'Chopinzee'. Less well known was that, in his spare time while living in London, he often went for walks around Golden Square with 'a fortune in precious stones concealed in the lining of his battered old hat'.[27]

Colin MacInnes' friend, the writer, jazz singer and bisexual bohemian George Melly, made Soho his adoptive, nocturnal home from the mid-1940s onwards. After wartime service in the Royal Navy he found employment at E. L. T. Mesens's London Gallery in Beak Street, and became involved in a love triangle with Mesens and his wife. Melly's Soho was 'a scruffy, warm, belching, argumentative, groping, spewing-up, cadging, toothbrush-in-pocket, warm-beer-gulping world'. He joined Mick Mulligan's Magnolia Jazz Band, performing 1920s jazz classics, 'using Benzedrine to stay up all night and occasionally sleeping in brothels'.[28] He was a stalwart of the Colony Room, becoming an archetype of Soho in the 1950s in the process. Melly met his first wife, Elizabeth Victoria (Vicky) Vaughan, a fashion model, in a Soho club, but she left him after only a year for a man with whom Melly himself had already had an affair.

Soho's reputation for jazz music was further enhanced by Ronnie Scott, who was playing the saxophone professionally in Soho at the age of only sixteen and gained his first experience in running a jazz club at Club Eleven on Great Windmill Street in 1949. In 1959 he established Ronnie Scott's in Gerrard Street, which quickly turned into Britain's most famous jazz venue, attracting star performers including Dizzy Gillespie, Dexter Gordon, Coleman Hawkins and Stan Getz. The club attracted prominent guests including royalty, politicians and show-business stars, who enjoyed the relaxed atmosphere and the fact that Scott never attempted to capitalise on their presence.

Soho not only inspired actors, musicians and writers, but also artists. The painter and illustrator John Minton, who possessed an 'infectious gaiety' and made no secret of his homosexuality, often frequented Soho with 'Johnny's Club', the entourage of young arts students he took under his wing. Soho was the perfect setting for the wealthy and generous artist who 'lived always in the moment, driven urgently by a need for company and change'.[29]

Francis Bacon, enfant terrible and famous painter, settled in London in 1928 after drifting through Paris and Berlin where the decadent nightlife of Weimar Germany left a lasting impression on his life. He first came to fame in London as an interior designer, receiving celebrated commissions such as designing

Ronnie Scott playing the saxophone at the gala opening of the Ronnie Scott Club, 1961.

furniture for the kitchen of politician R. A. Butler. He taught himself how to paint and, drawing on the work of artists such as the Russian filmmaker Sergei Eisenstein as inspiration, he developed the style of painting which would make him one of 'the most powerful and horrifying' painters of the second half of the twentieth century. His *Three Studies for Figures at the Base of a Crucifixion* brought him instant notoriety in 1945, and his subsequent work was a reflection of 'his belief that the image should act as an assault on the nervous system rather than a stimulus for the intellect'.[30]

Soho remained the main setting for Bacon's life of eccentric squalor throughout the 1950s. A day after the Colony Room Club's opening, the notorious Muriel Belcher employed him to bring in people. Regulars at the club included a circle of Bacon's artist friends, among them Lucian Freud, Michael Andrews and Frank Auerbach.

The artist and writer Nina Hamnett, a 'natural rebel' with flamboyant behaviour, was one of the best-known bohemians of the inter-war period in both London and Paris. She knew both Picasso and Sickert, and modelled for Modigliani who, she would say, 'said I had the best tits in Europe'. After the end of her marriage in 1917 she took a string of lovers, apparently preferring boxers and sailors, as 'they go away'. Her career began to decline, and she spent much of the 1930s and 1940s in Fitzrovia and Soho, succumbing to alcoholism and incontinence. A regular at the French pub, the Caves de France and the Colony Room until Muriel Belcher banned her, she was always willing to tell another anecdote for the next drink. In 1956 she fell from the window of her room and was impaled on the railings beneath, only days after an unflattering radio play about her. The coroner recorded a verdict of accidental death, although her few remaining friends thought it was more likely to have been suicide.

The photographer and painter John Deakin, who 'when drunk was a monster', worked as staff photographer of *Vogue* magazine. He took pictures of many writers, artists, poets, actors and popular

Francis Bacon and Muriel Belcher in the Colony Room. Photograph by Peter Stark, 1975.

entertainers of the 1950s, including Yves Montand, Pablo Picasso, Maria Callas and Dylan Thomas. However, some of his best portraits were of his friends in the haunts they frequented together in Soho. George Melly described him as 'a vicious little drunk of such inventive malice and implacable bitchiness that it's surprising he didn't choke on his own venom'.[31] The Colony Room in Dean Street was his favourite drinking den until its proprietor Muriel Belcher barred him. She featured in many of his photographs, as did John Minton and Francis Bacon. After his death in 1972, his life's work was discovered under his bed in Soho by Bruce Bernard, who later staged the exhibition *John Deakin: The Salvage of a Photographer* at the V&A.

The sleazy world of Soho often produced its own celebrities. Paul Raymond, former theatrical impresario and at one time the richest man in Britain, became famous when he opened the Raymond Revuebar in Soho in 1957. Born Geoffrey Quinn to a middle-class Catholic family, he had adopted his new name on account of its saucy French associations. Before turning his attention to stage management he had been involved in London's black market and gained credibility among the gangsters of Soho's criminal underworld. His dark and conservative suits made clear he wanted to be regarded as a respectable businessman, but his hairstyle and pencil moustache betrayed him as the archetypical spiv.

The Revuebar's profits – which were, according to Raymond, ten times the earnings of the prime minister – enabled him to take over the Windmill Theatre, and it was Raymond, the 'Godfather of Porn', who made nudity almost respectable. His financial success was, however, not matched by a happy private life. Divorced by his wife for adultery and having lost one of his children due to a drugs overdose he died a virtual recluse, lamenting that 'people only like him for his money'.[32]

Like the Raymond Revuebar, many of Soho's infamous drinking haunts were defined by the colourful personalities of their proprietors. It was the energy and humour of Muriel Belcher that turned the Colony Room Club into one of the most popular drinking dens for Soho's bohemians. She ruled over 'its shabby bamboo-clad bar like a monarch' and her 'strong, Sephardic profile' was reminiscent of a hawk.[33] She could be kind and warm-hearted to those customers she took a liking to, but she was also infamous for her insults and rude behaviour. She liked to call her favourite male customers her 'daughters', but strangers who stepped into the club would often be told in no uncertain terms to turn on their heels. George Melly thought she was 'a handsome Jewish dyke' and 'a benevolent witch', who 'was like a great cook, working with the ingredients of people and drink. And she loved money'.[34]

Norman Balon, the famously grumpy landlord of the Coach and Horses who had worked behind the bar of the pub since 1943, commented on why the pub was popular: 'It's me. A pub is a reflection of a landlord's personality and I can't stand bores.'[35] His autobiography is fittingly titled *You're Barred You Bastards*.

Not all Sohoites famous in the local area were well known beyond the streets of the West End. Solomon Milbourne, nicknamed 'the Turk', had come to London from Poland in 1897 and traded as a costumier, until his business in Berwick Street and Wardour Street went bankrupt in 1929. This 'Yiddisher "Champagne Charlie"' enjoyed showing off his wealth, and was 'the first in Berwick Street to appear with a Rolls-Royce and a chauffeur . . . He swaggered along the road, flaunting a loud check waistcoat across a broad expanse of chest, sporting an ivory-handled walking stick and cigar. He was on friendly terms with the poor residents, never giving any "side", despite his success, until one day he went bust'.[36] His was only one of the many rags-to-riches stories of Soho which ended with a return to rags.

There were many more Soho residents whose unique personalities shaped the area, and this chapter has tried to provide at least a flavour of the wealth of the district's history. Soho's central location in the West End, its mix of poverty and

'An Arab Café.' Plate in G. R. Sims (ed.), *Living London. Its Work and its Play. Its Humour and its Pathos. Its Sights and its Scenes*, Cassell 1901.

wealth, its allure as a dangerous yet attractive part of London's underworld, its growing world of daytime businesses and night-time entertainment attracted the many revellers and bohemians who often sought refuge from the strict social norms of Victorian and early twentieth-century London.

The revellers mixed with the many refugees from across the world that made Soho their home away from home, and it is this mix of the women and men of Soho that lies at the heart of the area's enduring popularity across the globe. The Soho of today is in many ways shaped by the history of its streets, its enterprise, entertainment and residents since Victorian times, and traces of this past are still evident all over Soho.

Photograph of St Anne's Court, running between Dean Street and Wardour Street, in St John Adcock (ed.), *Wonderful London*, 1928. The caption rather pompously states that the 'narrow, untidy, gloomy' street 'typifies the area chosen for their abode by a large proportion of London's foreign residents ... but the film industry has also gone to earth in these warrens, for reasons best known to itself'.

Chapter 6   **Legacy**

In his 1969 book *Skin Deep in Soho*, Richard Worthy writes that 'Soho is a notorious place and there is nothing left to say about it'. Of course much has been said and written about Soho since then, and the area's history is as fascinating as ever. Worthy's views on the character of the area were as true in the mid-nineteenth century as they were in the mid-twentieth century, and indeed they are still relevant today: 'Soho has many ingredients. Crime, Club, Café, Pub, Spieler, Stripper, Drummer, Whizzer, Slapper, Shmatter, Song-Plugger, Tailor and Cutter ... Soho belongs to the people who work there.'[1]

This book has explored Soho's streets, its businesses, its world of entertainment as well as its people, and it is the unique mix of all of these throughout history that explains why Soho is as fascinating today as it was 200 years ago. Although the number of residents steadily declined in the twentieth century, Soho continued to be an important social, cultural and economic centre of London. Nowhere was Britain's post-war youth revolution more evident than in the coffee bars that sprang up in 1950s Soho. Teddy boys, Rockers and skiffle fans could spend hours listening to the latest Elvis record on the jukebox for the price of a cup of frothy coffee. This was a nationwide phenomenon, of course, but as one former jiver remembered, 'Soho was simply the Mecca. It had the best skiffle, the best rock, and the best jazz'.[2] The 1960s and Swinging London added the new, and revolutionary, discotheque, which arguably transformed Soho's and London's nightlife into an experience free of class or race boundaries. Punks in the 1970s and New Romantics in the 1980s were just as much at home in Soho as the Teddy boys had been before them.

Today, many walking tours take place through the streets of Soho, exploring similar themes to those in this book – but for some Londoners in times gone by, the streets could be rather less enjoyable. From the 1960s onwards Soho's streets were patrolled by traffic wardens, who faced circumstances different from those in other parts of London. Tom Cooke, one of London's first traffic wardens, remembered:

> I patrolled Soho, which meant that I was always going to have more than my fair share of problems, because it was quite a rough area in those days. I had an orange hit me on the face thrown from eight storeys up – walnuts, stones, the lot. Once I was cornered in an alleyway by a doorman about 8-foot wide and thought that was the end of me but he changed his mind after I thought he was going to do me in.[3]

Soho has retained its reputation as a potentially dangerous place to this day. There is, however, much talk about the decline of the area's character due to gentrification, redevelopment and rising rents, as well as the fear that this will lead to the exodus of the remaining traditional businesses and the colourful communities. But the strong impressions that history has left on the area – with its fair share of wars, crime and poverty, as well as diversity, the pursuit of pleasure and entertainment – will be very hard to erase. Concerns over the decline of the area go as far back as the eighteenth century, and yet Soho has prevailed throughout time. It survived the Blitz, as well as the threat of wholesale demolition by 1970s planners who dreamed of a 'dystopian wasteland of fast-flowing traffic lanes, aerial walkways and tower-blocks'.[4]

While Soho increasingly caters for the wealthy, the area has not forgotten about the less fortunate. Many of Soho's charitable

The House of Barnabas, Greek Street. This grand eighteenth-century house became home to the St Barnabas charity in 1862. Lettering spelling out 'House of Charity' can still be seen on the side of the building. Today the House of Barnabas maintains its charitable role, providing a not-for-profit members club to help the homeless.

View of Chinatown, Soho, at night. 6 December 2013.

institutions that developed in the nineteenth century to tackle the widespread poverty continue to thrive. Greek Street, notorious as 'the worst street in the West End of London' in the early twentieth century, has also been home to the House of St Barnabas charity organisation since 1862. It resides in the eighteenth-century home of Richard Beckford, brother of William Beckford, London Mayor of London, and the grand building retains some of London's best surviving examples of rococo interiors. The House of Charity (as the House of Barnabas was originally known) had been founded in the 1840s to provide 'temporary relief to as many destitute cases as possible, and a Christian effect on the poor population'.[5] Since 2013 the building has also been hosting a 'dynamic, not-for-profit members club' to support London's homeless back into work. The club 'is demolishing stereotypes around the idea of exclusivity' by offering a mix of heritage, contemporary art and music unique to Soho.[6] This is just one example of the continuation of long-established efforts in Soho to address the problems of the area.

Although the threats of redevelopment and gentrification to the character of Soho are very real in the twenty-first century, its unique atmosphere has faced similar challenges in the past, and the people of Soho are unlikely to accept the loss of the district's heritage without a fight. In its past Soho has embraced inevitable change, and although many of Soho's traditional businesses and residents have moved on, the cosmopolitan character of the area and its status as a multicultural and tolerant, if at times somewhat sleazy, hub of music, arts and entertainment will surely prevail for future generations.

Notes

1. Introducing Soho

1. John Galsworthy, in Weinreb 2010, p. 845.
2. Burke 1915, p. 253.
3. MacInnes 1959, p. 307.
4. Norman and Bernard 1966, p. 4.
5. Casanova, in Summers 1989, p. 59.
6. Ransome 2002, p. 102.
7. Tames 2009, p. 8.
8. Black 1994, p. 36.
9. Ibid., p. 30.
10. Ibid., p. 31.
11. Ibid., p. 28.
12. Farson 1993, p. 50.
13. Anna Clerke, in Weinreb 2010, p. 845; Elizabeth Price and Elizabeth Flint, in Summers 1989, p. 107.
14. White 2008, p. 312.
15. *Illustrated London News*, 7 June 1851.

2. The Streets and Squares of Soho

1. Sherwell 1901, p. 1.
2. White 2008, p. 104.
3. G. R. Sims, cited in Chancellor 1931, p. 4.
4. Clayton 2005, p. 55.
5. John Nash, in Weinreb 2010, p. 685.
6. Truslove & Hanson 1911, Preface.
7. White 2008, p. 116.
8. Hollis and Wooding 1983.
9. Rimbault 1895, p. 92.
10. Walkowitz 2012, p. 23.
11. Thomas Frost, *Forty Years' Recollections*, 1880, cited in White 2007, p. 142.
12. Quoted in Summers 1989, p. 156.
13. Cardwell, Freeman and Wilton 1903, p. 29.
14. Rimbault 1895, p. 141.
15. Chancellor 1931, p. 1.
16. Humphries and Taylor 1986, p. 128.
17. John Strype, *Survey of the Cities of London and Westminster*, 1720. Available from https://www.hrionline.ac.uk/strype/TransformServlet?page=book6_086.

18. Quoted in White 2008, p. 105.
19. E. D. Glinert, 'West End Chronicles', 2008, in Reyes 2009, p. 119.
20. Humphries and Taylor 1986, p. 31.
21. Walkowitz 2012, p. 23.
22. E. D. Glinert, 'West End Chronicles', 2008, in Reyes 2009, p. 133.
23. Halasz 2010, p. 114 and p. 116.
24. Harold P. Clunn, cited in Walkowitz 2012, p. 20.
25. Walkowitz 2012, p. 20.
26. Quoted in Summers 1989, p. 126.
27. Goldsmith 1947, p. 166.
28. St Anne's, in Truslove & Hanson 1898.
29. Quoted in Truslove & Hanson 1911, p. 24.
30. Rimbault 1895, p. 124.
31. Walkowitz 2012, p. 21.

3. Making a Living

1. Arthur Ransome, *Bohemia in London*, 1907, pp.110–17, cited in Walkowitz 2012, p. 13.
2. Walkowitz 2012, p. 156.
3. Quoted in Walkowitz 2012, p. 54.
4. Leigh Hunt, 1861, cited in Summers 1989, p. 133.
5. Quoted in Summers 1989, p. 133.
6. Sherwell 1901, p. 7.
7. John Hollingshead, *Ragged London in 1861*, 1861, cited in Walkowitz 2012, p. 149.
8. Rimbault 1895, p. 178.
9. Walkowitz 2012, p. 144.
10. Quoted in Walkowitz 2012, p. 144 and p. 146.
11. Lewis 1965, p. 83.
12. Cole 1921, p. 21.
13. Woolf 1979, p. 135.
14. Benjamin 1930, p. 180.
15. Quoted in Walkowitz 2012, p. 171.
16. Black 1994, p. 61.
17. Quoted in Walkowitz 2012, p. 171.
18. Jackson 1946, p. 44.
19. Ibid., p. 131.
20. Walkowitz 2012, p. 157.
21. Henrey 1953, p. 100.
22. Jackson 1946, foreword.
23. Goldsmith 1947, p. 174.
24. Jackson 1946, p. 28.
25. Black 1994, p. 74.
26. Cardwell 2011, p. 189, cited in Walkowitz 2012, p. 30.
27. Quoted in Summers 1989, p. 180.
28. Hutton 2013, p. 127.
29. Jackson 1946, pp. 48–49.
30. Norman and Bernard 1966, p. 4.
31. Tietjen 1956, p. 18.

32. Truslove & Hanson 1911, p. 20.
33. Cited in Chancellor 1931, p. 4.
34. White 2008, p. 261.
35. Jackson 1946, foreword.
36. Daniel Farson, *Soho in the Fifties*, 1988, cited in Reyes 2009, p. 122.
37. Jackson 1946, foreword.
38. Reyes 2009, p. 122.
39. White 2008, p. 275.
40. Jackson 1946, p. 113.
41. 'Meet the Spiv', *Tailor & Cutter*, 15 August 1947, p. 561.
42. White 2007, p. 303.
43. Morton 2008, p. 10.
44. White 2007, p. 305.
45. Walter, *My Secret Life*, vol. 3, Ch. XII, 1888–94, pp. 524–25, cited in White 2007, p. 306.
46. Walkowitz 2012, p. 314.
47. An old Soho resident, quoted in Tony Aldous, *The Illustrated London News Book of London's Villages*, 1980, p. 242, cited in White 2008, p. 322.
48. Farson 1993, p. 50.
49. Hollis and Wooding 1983, p. 228.
50. Percy Savage, cited in Morton 2008, p. 12.
51. Morton 2008, p. 13.
52. Ibid., p. 15.
53. Quoted in ibid., pp. 28–29.
54. Quoted in ibid., p. 34.
55. Ibid., p. 34.
56. *Sunday Pictorial*, quoted in ibid., p. 35.
57. Ibid, p. 37.
58. Burke 1919, p. 62.
59. Eliza Cook, cited in Walkowitz 2012, p. 97.
60. Charles Booth, *Life and Labour of the People in London*, 1892–97, cited in Walkowitz 2012, p. 98.
61. H. G. Wells, cited in Walkowitz 2012, p. 102.
62. Charles Booth, *Life and Labour of the People in London*, 1892–97, cited in Walkowitz 2012, p. 103.

4. World of Arts and Entertainment

1. Truslove & Hanson 1911, preface.
2. Christopher Gibbs, quoted in Levy 2002, p. 50.
3. Robert Machray, quoted in Walkowitz 2012, p. 13.
4. Walkowitz 2012, p. 15.
5. White 2007, p. 286.
6. Tames 2009, p. 147.
7. Roger Dobson, 'Machen, Arthur Llewelyn Jones (1863–1947)', *Oxford Dictionary of National Biography*, Oxford

University Press 2004; online edn, January 2006 [http://www.oxforddnb. com/view/article/37711, accessed 16 January 2017].

8. Mary Anne Duignan (aka Chicago May), *Chicago May, Her Story, by the Queen of Crooks*, 1928, quoted in White 2008, p. 329.

9. Walkowitz 2012, p. 113.

10. *Survey of London, Volumes 33 and 34*, Gerrard Street Area, *British History Online* [http://www.british-history. ac.uk/survey-london/vols33-4/pp384-411#h3-0019, accessed 16 January 2017].

11. *The Times*, 18 September 1890, p. 5.

12. Quoted in Walkowitz 2012, p. 116.

13. Chancellor 1931, p.1.

14. Quoted in Walkowitz 2012, p. 119.

15. Quoted in ibid., p. 119.

16. Quoted in ibid., p. 246.

17. Levy 2002, p. 52.

18. White 2008, p. 338.

19. Tames 2009, p. 150.

20. Ibid., p. 114.

21. W. Macqueen-Pope, 'Old-Time Magic of the Empire', *Everybody's*, 31 December 1949, cited in Walkowitz 2012, p. 55.

22. Weinreb 2010, p. 16.

23. Daniel Joseph Kirwan, 1870, cited in Walkowitz 2012, p. 55.

24. Quoted in Tames 2009, p. 63.

25. Hutton 2013, p. 23.

26. White 2008, p. 335.

27. Quoted in ibid., p. 340.

28. Quoted in Ross and Clark 2008, p. 285.

29. Arthur Sherwell, cited in White 2008, p. 329.

30. Clayton 2005, p. 72.

31. Quoted in Miles 2011, p. 37.

32. Hoare 1997, p. 5.

33. Michael Holroyd, 'John, Augustus Edwin (1878–1961)', *Oxford Dictionary of National Biography*, Oxford University Press 2004; online edn, May 2006 [http://www.oxforddnb. com/view/article/34196, accessed 9 January 2017].

34. White 2008, p. 333.

35. Richard Davenport-Hines, 'Meyrick , Kate Evelyn (1875–1933)', *Oxford Dictionary of National Biography*, Oxford University Press 2004; online edn, January 2013 [http:// www.oxforddnb.com/view/ article/66827, accessed 9 December 2016].

36. Quoted in Walkowitz 2012, p. 221.

37. Quoted in ibid., p.232.

38. Ibid., p. 234.
39. Leonard Feather and *London Week* quoted in Walkowitz 2012, p. 237.
40. Billy Amstell, cited in Walkowitz 2012, p. 239.
41. Quoted in Walkowitz 2012, p. 240.
42. Quoted in Walkowitz 2012, p. 230.
43. Quoted in White 2008, p. 337.
44. Quoted in Miles 2011, p. 35.
45. Parkin 2013, p. 3.
46. ibid.
47. Tames 2009, p. 40.
48. Quoted in Ross and Clark 2008, p. 285.
49. Halasz 2010, p. 187.
50. Ibid., p. 169.
51. Ibid., p. 172 and p. 187.
52. Ibid., p. 176 and p. 184.
53. Porter 2000, p. 443.

5. Women and Men of Soho

1. Quoted in Summers 1989, p. 194.
2. John Hollingshead, *Ragged London*, 1861, cited in Summers 1989, p. 111.
3. MacInnes 1959, cited in Reyes 2009, p. 122.
4. Norman and Bernard 1966, p. 4.
5. Quoted in White 2008, p. 108.
6. Quoted in White 2008, p. 108.
7. Quoted in Walkowitz 2012, p. 121.
8. Tames 2009, p. 103.
9. Truslove & Hanson 1911, p. 43.
10. Charles Booth, *Life and Labour of the People in London*, 1892–97, cited in Walkowitz 2012, p. 151.
11. Truslove & Hanson 1911, p. 43.
12. Quoted in Black 1994, p. 25.
13. Quoted in ibid., p. 22.
14. Peter Thomson, 'Kean, Edmund (1787–1833)', *Oxford Dictionary of National Biography*, Oxford University Press 2004; online edn, January 2015 [http://www.oxforddnb.com/view/article/15204, accessed 18 November 2016].
15. M. Glen Wilson, 'Kean, Charles John (1811–1868)', *Oxford Dictionary of National Biography*, Oxford University Press 2004; online edn, January 2008 [http://www.oxforddnb.com/view/article/15203, accessed 14 October 2016].
16. Trewin 1967, p. 225.
17. John Russell Stephens, 'Kemble, Charles (1775–1854)', *Oxford Dictionary of National Biography*, Oxford

University Press 2004; online edn, January 2008 [http://www.oxforddnb.com/view/article/15316, accessed 14 October 2016].

18. J. T. Grein quoted in Tames 2009, p. 100.

19. Barbara Belford, 'Stoker, Abraham (1847–1912)', *Oxford Dictionary of National Biography*, Oxford University Press 2004 [http://www.oxforddnb.com/view/article/38012, accessed 4 November 2016].

20. Quoted in Morton 2008, p. 80.

21. Philip Hoare, 'Carleton, Billie (1896–1918)', *Oxford Dictionary of National Biography*, Oxford University Press 2004; online edn, September 2010 [http://www.oxforddnb.com/view/article/64888, accessed 14 October 2016].

22. Thomas Carlyle, cited in Michael Slater, 'Dickens, Charles John Huffam (1812–1870)', *Oxford Dictionary of National Biography*, Oxford University Press 2004; online edn, September 2014 [http://www.oxforddnb.com/view/

article/7599, accessed 18 November 2016].

23. Grevel Lindop, 'Quincey, Thomas Penson De (1785–1859)', *Oxford Dictionary of National Biography*, Oxford University Press 2004; online edn, 2004 [http://www.oxforddnb.com/view/article/7524, accessed 25 October 2016].

24. Owen Dudley Edwards, 'Wilde, Oscar Fingal O'Flahertie Wills (1854–1900)', *Oxford Dictionary of National Biography*, Oxford University Press 2004; online edn, September 2012 [http://www.oxforddnb.com/view/article/29400, accessed 25 October 2016].

25. Lyndall Gordon, 'Woolf, (Adeline) Virginia (1882–1941)', *Oxford Dictionary of National Biography*, Oxford University Press 2005 [http://www.oxforddnb.com/view/article/37018, accessed 4 November 2016].

26. Colin MacInnes, *England, Half English*, cited in Jerry White, 2008, p. 340.

27. Bushell 1983, p. 35.

28. Philip Hoare, 'Melly, (Alan) George Heywood (1926–2007)', *Oxford Dictionary*

of National Biography, Oxford University Press 2011; online edn, May 2011 [http://www.oxforddnb.com/view/article/98953, accessed 11 November 2016].

29. Michael Middleton, 'Minton, (Francis) John (1917–1957)', *Oxford Dictionary of National Biography*, Oxford University Press 2004; online edn, October 2006 [http://www.oxforddnb.com/view/article/35041, accessed 25 November 2016].

30. James Hyman, 'Bacon, Francis (1909–1992)', *Oxford Dictionary of National Biography*, Oxford University Press 2004; online edn, January 2011 [http://www.oxforddnb.com/view/article/50800, accessed 11 October 2016].

31. Quoted in Tames 2009, p. 56.

32. Dennis Barker, 'Raymond, Paul (1925–2008)', *Oxford Dictionary of National Biography*, Oxford University Press 2012; online edition, September 2013 [http://www.oxforddnb.com/view/article/100106, accessed 21 October 2016].

33. Summers 1989, p. 192.

34. Quoted in Tames 2009, p. 21.

35. Quoted in ibid., p. 47.

36. Walkowitz 2012, p. 163.

6. Legacy

1. Wortley 1969, p. 75.

2. Summers 1989, p. 195.

3. Quoted in Humphries and Taylor 1986, p. 73.

4. Tames 2009, p. 8.

5. Weinreb 2010, p. 419.

6. The House of St Barnabas, London, available at https://hosb.org.uk/our-members-club/#about-our-club.

Further Reading

Books

Allen 1839: Thomas Allen, continued by Thomas Wright, *The History and Antiquities of London, Westminster and Southwark*, vol. IV, G. Virtue 1839.

Benjamin 1930: Thelma Benjamin, *A Shopping Guide to London*, R. M. McBride 1930.

Black 1994: Gerry Black, *Living Up West*, London Museum of Jewish Life 1994.

Burke 1915: Thomas Burke, *Nights in Town: A London Autobiography*, Allen & Unwin 1915.

Burke 1919: Thomas Burke, *Out and About: A Note-Book of London in War-Time*, Allen & Unwin 1919.

Bushell 1983: Peter Bushell, *London's Secret History*, Constable 1983.

Cardwell 2011: Rev. J.H. Cardwell, et al., *Two Centuries of Soho: Its Institutions, Firms and Amusements*, 1st edition Truslove & Hanson 1898; current edition British Library 2011.

Cardwell, Freeman and Wilton 1903: Rev. J. H. Cardwell, H. B. Freeman, G. C. Wilton et. al., *Men and Women of Soho, Famous and Infamous*, London, Truslove & Hanson 1903.

Chancellor 1931: E. Beresford Chancellor, *The Romance of Soho*, Country Life 1931.

Clayton 2005: Antony Clayton, *Decadent London: Fin de Siècle City*, Historical Publications 2005.

Cole 1921: Sophie Cole, *The Lure of Old London*, Mills & Boon 1921.

Edmonds 1988: Mark Edmonds, *Inside Soho*, Nicholson 1988.

Farson 1993: Daniel Farson, *The Guilded Gutter Life of Francis*

Bacon, Pantheon 1993.

Goldsmith 1947: Margaret Goldsmith, *Soho Square*, Sampson Low, Marston & Co. Ltd 1947.

Halasz 2010: Piri Halasz, *A Swinger's Guide to London*, original edition Coward-McCann, 1967, current edition iUniverse 2010.

Henrey 1953: Mrs Robert Henrey, *Madeleine Grown Up*, Dutton 1953.

Hoare 1997: Philip Hoare, *Wilde's Last Stand*, Arcade 1997.

Hollis and Wooding 1983: Henry Hollis and Dan Wooding, *Farewell Leicester Square*, Stuart Titles 1983.

Humphries and Taylor 1986: Steve Humphries and John Taylor, *The Making of Modern London*, 1945–1985, Sidgwick & Jackson 1986.

Hutton 2013: Mike Hutton, *The Story of Soho: The Windmill Years, 1932–1964*, Amberley 2013.

Jackson 1946: Stanley Jackson, *An Indiscreet Guide to Soho*, Muse Arts 1946.

Levy 2002: Shawn Levy, *Ready, Steady, Go! Swinging London and the Invention of Cool*, Fourth Estate 2003.

Lewis 1965: Chaim Lewis, *A Soho Address*, Gollancz 1965.

MacInnes 1959: Colin MacInnes, *Absolute Beginners*, MacGibbon & Kee 1959, current edition Allison & Busby 2001.

Miles 2011: Barry Miles, *London Calling*, Atlantic Books 2011.

Morton 2008: James Morton, *Gangland Soho*, Piatkus 2008.

Norman and Bernard 1966: Frank Norman and Jeffrey Bernard, *Soho Night & Day*, Secker & Warburg 1966.

Parkin 2013: Sophie Parkin, *The Colony Room Club: A History of Bohemian Soho*, Palmtree 2013.

Porter 2000: Roy Porter, *London, A Social History*, Penguin 2000.

Ransome 2002: Arthur Ransome, *Bohemia in London*, original edition Chapman & Hall 1907, current edition Amazon Publications 2002.

Reyes 2009: Heather Reyes (ed.), *City-lit London*, Oxygen Books 2009.

Rimbault 1895: Edward Francis Rimbault, *Soho and its Associations, Historical, Literary and Artistic*, Dulau 1895.

Ross and Clark 2008: Cathy Ross and John Clark, *London: The*

Illustrated History, Penguin 2011.

Sherwell 1901: Arthur Sherwell, *Life in West London: A Study and a Contrast*, Methuen & Co. 1901.

Summers 1989: Judith Summers, *Soho*, Bloomsbury Publishing 1989.

Tames 2009: Richard and Sheila Tames, *Covent Garden and Soho: The Illustrated A–Z Historical Guide*, Historical Publications 2009.

Tietjen 1956: Arthur Tietjen, *Soho: London's Vicious Circle*, Allan Wingate 1956.

Trewin 1967: J. C. Trewin (ed.), *The Journal of William Charles Macready, 1832–1851*, Longman 1967.

Truslove & Hanson 1911: *Twenty Years in Soho: A Review of the Work of the Church in the Parish of St Anne's, Soho, from 1891 to 1911*, Truslove & Hanson 1911.

Truslove & Hanson 1898: *Two Centuries of Soho*, Truslove & Hanson 1898.

Wagner 1925: Leopold Wagner, *More London Inns and Taverns*, Allen & Unwin 1925.

Walkowitz 2012: Judith Walkowitz, *Nights Out*, Yale University Press 2012.

Weinreb, 2010: Ben Weinreb et al., *The London Encyclopaedia*, 3rd edition, Macmillan 2010.

White 2007: Jerry White, *London in the Nineteenth Century*, Cape 2007.

White 2008: Jerry White, *London in the Twentieth Century*, Vintage 2008.

Woolf 1979: Virginia Woolf, *The Diary of Virginia Woolf, Volume 1, 1915–1919*, ed. Anne Olivier Bell, Penguin 1979.

Wortley 1969: Richard Wortley, *Skin Deep in Soho*, Jarrolds 1969.

Online articles

Barker, Dennis, 'Raymond, Paul (1925–2008)', *Oxford Dictionary of National Biography*, Oxford University Press January 2012; online edn, September 2013 [http://www.oxforddnb.com/view/article/100106, accessed 21 October 2016].

Belford, Barbara, 'Stoker, Abraham (1847–1912)', *Oxford Dictionary of National Biography*, Oxford University Press 2004 [http://www.oxforddnb.com/view/article/38012, accessed 4 November 2016].

Booth, Michael R., 'Terry, Dame Ellen Alice (1847–1928)', *Oxford Dictionary of National Biography*, Oxford

University Press 2004; online edn, January 2011 [http://www.oxforddnb.com/view/article/36460, accessed 21 October 2016].

Bowness, Sophie, 'Nicholson, Sir William Newzam Prior (1872–1949)', *Oxford Dictionary of National Biography*, Oxford University Press 2004; online edn, May 2008 [http://www.oxforddnb.com/view/article/35233, accessed 16 January 2017].

Davenport-Hines, Richard, 'Meyrick, Kate Evelyn (1875–1933)', *Oxford Dictionary of National Biography*, Oxford University Press 2004; online edn, January 2013 [http://www.oxforddnb.com/view/article/66827, accessed 9 December 2016].

Davies, Robertson, 'Irving, Sir Henry (1838–1905)', *Oxford Dictionary of National Biography*, Oxford University Press 2004; online edn, January 2008 [http://www.oxforddnb.com/view/article/34116, accessed 14 October 2016]

Dobson, Roger, 'Machen, Arthur Llewelyn Jones (1863–1947)', *Oxford Dictionary of National Biography*, Oxford University Press 2004; online edn, January 2006 [http://www.oxforddnb.com/view/article/37711, accessed 16 January 2017].

Edwards, Owen Dudley, 'Wilde, Oscar Fingal O'Flahertie Wills (1854–1900)', *Oxford Dictionary of National Biography*, Oxford University Press 2004; online edn, September 2012 [http://www.oxforddnb.com/view/article/29400, accessed 25 October 2016].

Gordon, Lyndall, 'Woolf, (Adeline) Virginia (1882–1941)', *Oxford Dictionary of National Biography*, Oxford University Press 2005 [http://www.oxforddnb.com/view/article/37018, accessed 4 November 2016].

Hoare, Philip, 'Carleton, Billie (1896–1918)', *Oxford Dictionary of National Biography*, Oxford University Press 2004; online edn, September 2010 [http://www.oxforddnb.com/view/article/64888, accessed 14 October 2016].

Hoare, Philip, 'Melly, (Alan) George Heywood (1926–2007)', *Oxford Dictionary of National Biography*, Oxford University Press 2011; online edn, May 2011 [http://www.oxforddnb.com/view/

article/98953, accessed 11 November 2016].

Hobsbawm, E. J. E., 'Marx, Karl Heinrich (1818–1883)', *Oxford Dictionary of National Biography*, Oxford University Press 2004; online edn, May 2015 [http://www.oxforddnb.com/view/article/39021, accessed 30 September 2015].

Holroyd, Michael, 'John, Augustus Edwin (1878–1961)', *Oxford Dictionary of National Biography*, Oxford University Press 2004; online edn, May 2006 [http://www.oxforddnb.com/view/article/34196, accessed 9 January 2017].

Hooker, Denise, 'Hamnett, Nina (1890–1956)', *Oxford Dictionary of National Biography*, Oxford University Press 2004 [http://www.oxforddnb.com/view/article/57344, accessed 25 November 2016].

Hyman, James, 'Bacon, Francis (1909–1992)', *Oxford Dictionary of National Biography*, Oxford University Press 2004; online edn, January 2011 [http://www.oxforddnb.com/view/article/50800, accessed 11 October 2016].

Jacobs, Arthur, 'Carte, Richard D'Oyly (1844–1901)', *Oxford Dictionary of National Biography*, Oxford University Press 2004; online edn, January 2008 [http://www.oxforddnb.com/view/article/32311, accessed 16 January 2017].

Kent, Charles, 'Kelly, Frances Maria (1790–1882)', rev. J. Gilliland, *Oxford Dictionary of National Biography*, Oxford University Press 2004; online edn, January 2008 [http://www.oxforddnb.com/view/article/15296, accessed 2 December 2015].

Knight, Joseph, 'Moore, Eleanora (1844/5–1869)', rev. J. Gilliland, *Oxford Dictionary of National Biography*, Oxford University Press 2004 [http://www.oxforddnb.com/view/article/19106, accessed 14 October 2016].

Lindop, Grevel, 'Quincey, Thomas Penson De (1785–1859)', *Oxford Dictionary of National Biography*, Oxford University Press 2004; online edn, 2004 [http://www.oxforddnb.com/view/article/7524, accessed 25 October 2016].

Middleton, Michael, 'Minton, (Francis) John (1917–1957)', *Oxford Dictionary of National Biography*, Oxford University Press 2004; online edn, October 2006 [http://www.oxforddnb.com/view/article/35041, accessed 25 November 2016].

Morgan, Alun, 'Scott, Ronald [Ronnie] (1927–1996)', *Oxford Dictionary of National Biography*, Oxford University Press 2004; online edn, May 2006 [http://www.oxforddnb.com/view/article/63995, accessed 11 November 2016].

Muir, Robin, 'Deakin, John (1912–1972)', *Oxford Dictionary of National Biography*, Oxford University Press 2004; online edn, January 2012 [http://www.oxforddnb.com/view/article/54351, accessed 25 November 2016.

Oxbury, H.F., 'Matthews, Jessie Margaret (1907–1981)', rev. *Oxford Dictionary of National Biography*, Oxford University Press 2004; online edn, Jan 2011 [http://www.oxforddnb.com/view/article/31425, accessed 18 October 2016].

Pimlott Baker, Anne, 'Barnby, Sir Joseph (1838–1896)', *Oxford Dictionary of National Biography*, Oxford University Press 2004 [http://www.oxforddnb.com/view/article/1465, accessed 11 November 2016].

Slater, Michael, 'Dickens, Charles John Huffam (1812–1870)', *Oxford Dictionary of National Biography*, Oxford University Press 2004; online edn, September 2014 [http://www.oxforddnb.com/view/article/7599, accessed 18 November 2016].

Survey of London, Volumes 33 and 34, Gerrard Street Area, *British History Online*, [http://www.british-history.ac.uk/survey-london/vols33-4/pp384-411#h3-0019, accessed 16 January 2017].

Stephens, John Russell, 'Kemble, Charles (1775–1854)', *Oxford Dictionary of National Biography*, Oxford University Press 2004; online edn, January 2008 [http://www.oxforddnb.com/view/article/15316, accessed 14 October 2016].

Thomson, Peter, 'Kean, Edmund (1787–1833)', *Oxford Dictionary of National Biography*, Oxford University Press 2004; online edn, January 2015 [http://www.oxforddnb.com/view/article/15204, accessed 18 November 2016].

Watts, Cedric, 'Conrad, Joseph (1857–1924)', *Oxford Dictionary of National Biography*, Oxford University

Press 2004; online edn, January 2011 [http://www.oxforddnb.com/view/article/32533, accessed 25 November 2016].

Wilmer, Val, 'Johnson, Kenrick Reginald Hijmans (1914–1941)', *Oxford Dictionary of National Biography*, Oxford University Press 2004; online edn, May 2006 [http://www.oxforddnb. com/view/article/74576, accessed 10 January 2017].

Wilson, M. Glen, 'Kean, Charles John (1811–1868)', *Oxford Dictionary of National Biography*, Oxford University Press 2004; online edn, January 2008 [http://www.oxforddnb.com/view/article/15203, accessed 14 October 2016].

Picture Credits

Acknowledgements

I am greatly indebted to the many historians and writers whose work I used to discover the complex and fascinating history of Soho. Naturally any errors in this book are my own.

I am also grateful to Robert Davies and Miranda Harrison at British Library Publishing for their advice and patience throughout the process of writing this book, as well as the friendly and supportive staff at the British Library Reading Rooms.

I would furthermore like to thank the history students at the University of Westminster who provided much of the inspiration for this book.

Finally, I would like to thank my family, especially Nelli, Richard, Fredy, Veronica, Quinn and Zoe, for their understanding and support.

Index

References in *italic* indicate pages on which illustrations appear

Carnaby Street 15, 48–50, *49*, 62, 129, 142
carpenters 60
Carrick, Edward 102
Casanova 8–12
Caterer Workers Union 139
Caves de France 34, 129, 158
celebrities 101, 107, 117, 135, 145; *see also*
    actors/actresses; *and under individual*
    names
Celoria, Eugenio *140*
Chan Nan *see* 'Brilliant Chang'
Chant, Mrs Ormiston 113
Charing Cross Road 21, 52, 54, 74, 107,
    119, 136
charity 166–69, *167*
Chelsea Setters 97
Chinatown 23, 30, 39, 41, 83, 107, 138, 149
Chinese communities 26, 92–93
    see also Chinatown
Chinese food/restaurants 41, 107, 138
cholera *13*, 14, 46–48, 109, 144, *145*
Churchill, Winston 113
cinemas 15, 19, 111, 125
Cinquevalli, Paul 108
Clarke, Edward Marmaduke 109
Clarkson, Willy 148–49
Clerke, Anna 18
clockmakers 60
Club 11 50, 156
Club 41 129
clubs 34, *44*, 83, 120–31; *see also* jazz clubs;
    nightclubs; *and under individual names*
Coach and Horses 21, 161
cocaine 91–92, 93, 122
coffee bars/houses 15, 39, 43, 45, 98,
    115–17, *116*, 165
Cole, Sophie 69
Colony Room Club 34, 128, 129, 155, 156,
    158, *159*, 160–61
Comer, Jack 84
Conrad, Joseph 102, 121, 153–54
Corinthian Bazaar and Exhibition Rooms
    108
Corio, Silvio 139
Cornelys, Theresa 8, *10*
Cortesi brothers 83
courtesans *see* prostitutes/prostitution
Coventry Street 21, 34, 55, 99, 125
Coward, Noël 129, 149
Crabtree club 120
Cranbourn Street 58
Crazy Gang 109
crime/criminal underworld 18–19, 81–86,
    85, 89, 97, 133, 160; *see also* drug
    trafficking
Crosse & Blackwell 19, 78

Crown pub 119
Crown Street (later Charing Cross Road) 52
Cuba Club 122
Cummins, Gordon Frederick 84
Cy Laurie's Jazz Club 50

d'Éon, Chevalier (later Chevalière d'Éon)
    11
D'Oyly Carte, Richard 33, 108, 146
Dankworth, John 50
De Beaumont, Mademoiselle *see* d'Éon,
    Chevalier
De Hems pub 119
De Pachmann, Vladimir 155
De Quincey, Thomas 151
De Souza, Yorke 126
Deakin, John 154, 158–60
Dean Street 28, 30–37, *38*, 102, *103*, 128,
    141, 146, 155, 160
Delysia, Alice 104
department stores 19, 62; *see also* Soho
    Bazaar
Dickens, Charles 33, 99, 146, *147*, 151
disease 87, 136; *see also* cholera
drinking clubs 83, 120–21, 125, 128, 161;
    see also clubs; pubs; *and under*
    individual names
drug trafficking 92–93
drugs 91–93, 121, 122, 149, 151, 155
Dutch communities 119

East India House 66
Empire Theatre 55, 88, *112*, 109, 111–13,
    114, *150*
Engels, Friedrich 139
entertainment industries 8, 19, 33, 55,
    57, 60, 62, 68, 72, 94–95, 97, 135,
    136, 144–46, 163; *see also* clubs;
    restaurants; theatres

Farson, Daniel 154
fascism 139–41
fashion 15, 48–50, *49*, 64, 68, 70, 80, 86, 97;
    see also rag trade; tailoring
Feather, Leonard 124
film industry 76, 78–80, 94
film stars 107, 131, 149–51; *see also* actors/
    actresses; *and under individual names*
First World War 23, 88, 92, 94, 120, 141
Flint, Elizabeth 18
Florence, the 101
43 Club 41, 121–22, 153, 154
French communities 7, 23, 26, 28, 31,
    33, 39, 41, 72, 109, 119, 138, 138
    businesses/trades of 34, 39, 43, 76,
    93, 99, 138

Johnson, Willie 92
journalists 85, 91, 146
Joynson-Hicks, Sir William 122

Kean, Charles 146
Kean, Edmund 146
Keeble Ltd. 35
Kelly, Miss Fanny 33, 146
Kemble, Charles 146
Kemble, Fanny 146
Kemp House 46
Kempton, Freda 93, 122
Kettner's 45, 99, *100*, 151
King Bomba's *140*, 141
Kingly Street 121, 122, 124
Krays, the 86

La Pompeati *see* Cornelys, Theresa
Laye, Evelyn 104
Leicester Fields (later Leicester Square)
    12, 58
Leicester House 12
Leicester Square (previously Leicester
    Fields) 19, *20*, 22, 55–57, *56*, 75,
    102, 109
leisure industry *see* entertainment industries
Leoni, Peppino 102, *103*, 104, 141
Lexington Street 46
Liberty 66–68, 67
Liberty, Arthur Lasenby 66
licensing laws 78, 88, 101, 115, 125, 128
Lisle Street 39, 41, 74
Little Crown Court 6
London Fascio 139–41
London Palladium 108–9
Lyceum Theatre 148
Lyon's Corner House 102

Maccioni, Alvaro 107
Macclesfield Street 119
Machen, Arthur 101
MacInnes, Colin 7–8, 21, 154–55
Macready, William Charles 146
Malatesta, Errico 139
Mandrake 128
markets 45–46, 59, 68–69, 72
Marks & Spencer 71
Marx, Karl 14, 31, 50, 102, 139, 144
masquerades 8, *10*
Matcham, Frank 108
Mather, Andrew 111
Matthews, Jessie 149–50
Maxim's 99
Meard Street 18, 21, 128
Melly, George 155–56, 160, 161
Messina brothers 18, 84

Meyrick, Kate 41, 121–22, 154
Mifsud, 'Big Frank' 18
Milbourne, Solomon 161
Minton, John 21, 156, 160
'Miss Kelly's Theatre' 146, *147*; *see also*
    Royalty Theatre
Moka Bar *116*
Monmouth House, Soho Square 8, 53
Mont Blanc Restaurant 39, 99, 102,
    153
Moore, Nelly 146
Morgue Club 121
Morioni's 76
Mozart 37, 43, 155
murders 83, 84, 87
Muriel's *see* Colony Room
Murray, Dalton 121
Murray's 120
music 117, 165; *see also under individual
    music types*
music halls 19, 87–88, 97, 108–9, 111;
    see also under individual names
music shops 46, 72, 80
musical-instrument makers 60
musicians 117, 155–56; *see also under
    individual names*
Mussolini, Benito 139–40

Nag's Head 48
Nest, the 121, 122, 124
New Compton Street 92
New Royalty Theatre (previously Soho
    Theatre) 33–34
Newman Street 60
newsagents 75, 76
Newton, Sir Isaac 12
Nicholson, William 99–101
nightclubs 15, 98, 122, *123*, 126; *see also
    under individual names*
1917 Club 39, 154
Nixey, W. G. 54
Noel Street 141
Novello 78
nude/erotic theatre performances 21, 59,
    113, 115, 160

Obscene Publications Act (1959) 89
Odeon cinema 19, 111
Old Compton Street 41–43, 99, 117, 119,
    141, 155
opium 149, 151
Oxford Street 62, 64, 69, 72
Oxford University Press 76

Palace Theatre 107, 108
Palladium *see* London Palladium